D0685531

Dedication

To Freda—for your undiluted eye
and unconventional leaps

Contents

Acknowledgments

Four of the long poems included in this volume—*The Mixer*; *Meditations On Civil Rights Activists*; *Martin*; and *For Conduct And Innocents*—are part of the Civil Rights Archives at Queens College (New York City), the school attended by Andrew Goodman, who was martyred, along with James Chaney and Michael Schwerner, by white supremacists in Philadelphia, Mississippi during freedom summer of 1964. These four poems join with other works of mine in the Civil Rights Archives, including the *Litany of Offense and Apology*, a mixture of poetry and prose that I wrote at the request of The Episcopal Church and that became part of the national Day of Repentance (October 4, 2008) when The Episcopal Church publicly apologized for its role in transatlantic slavery and related evils; and *Evanescence: The Elaine Race Massacre*, a prose piece on the large-scale massacre of African-Americans that occurred during the fall of 1919 in Phillips County, Arkansas along the Mississippi River Delta, an event whose murderous and legal importance has been conspicuously overlooked by American history but whose consequences are now being revealed to a broad audience.

For Conduct And Innocents, a drama in verse that covers the three years preceding the arrest by the Nazi Gestapo in 1943 of the 20th century theologian and martyr, Dietrich Bonhoeffer, has been employed for two separate commemorations on Bonhoeffer by Trinity Wall Street, New York City. At the 65th anniversary of Bonhoeffer's martyrdom, portions of *For Conduct And Innocents* were featured at an event held in April, 2010 by Trinity Wall Street that also consisted of several of his favorite hymns and scholarly commentaries and historical recollections on the theologian. In October, 2015, a complete, but abbreviated version of *For Conduct And Innocents* was prepared and staged as part of the 70th anniversary of

Bonhoeffer's martyrdom; approximately fifty performers participated in a multi-media event surrounding this drama in verse that included film, dance, opera and choral music, and the American premier of a musical setting for the lyrical poem, "Dream," written in 1943 by the teenage Jewish poet, Abramek Koplowicz, who perished at Auschwitz.

Over the course of five weeks during March and April, 2011, selections from the poem, *Meditations On Civil Rights Activists*, were read at St. Paul's Chapel in downtown New York City. Jazz and storytelling combined with the verse for presentations on Jonathan Daniels, W. E. B. Du Bois, James Weldon Johnson, Ida B. Wells-Barnett and Martin Luther King, Jr. An expanded and fuller version of the poem on Martin Luther King, Jr., as contained in *Meditations On Civil Rights Activists*, resulted in a longer verse piece, *Martin*, also part of this volume.

Selections of my poetry from *St. Paul's Chapel & Selected Shorter Poems*, a book published in 2006 and reprinted by St. Johann Press as a second edition in 2010, appear in this volume—an excerpt from "Reunited In Café Divino" functions as the epigraph for *Now And Then: Selected Longer Poems*, and "Night Call" introduces *Exile*. The signature poem for *St. Paul's Chapel & Selected Shorter Poems* has been used since 2002 as the memento card for visitors to the Chapel, which stood after the 9/11 attacks at Ground Zero and which became the 24/7 relief center for the recovery workers during the nine months of cleanup; the Chapel has served as a point of pilgrimage for several million people who have come to the World Trade Center site after the Chapel reopened to the public on September 11, 2002.

Of Time Divided is immediately preceded by an epigraph: Excerpt from "The Raising of Lazarus" in *The Poetry of Rilke* by Rainer Maria Rilke, translated and edited by Edward Snow. Translation copyright © 2009 by Edward Snow. Reprinted by permission of North Point Press, a division of Farrar, Straus and Giroux, LLC.

Sincere thanks and appreciation are hereby expressed to the editors of the following journals and internet sites in which passages from certain poems included in this book appeared:

Exile: BlazeVOX; Green Mountains Review
For Conduct And Innocents: International Poetry Review; RiverSedge
Home: BlazeVOX; Green Mountains Review
January 12th, 1967: Literary Matters; Streetlight; Waterways

Lawrence Joseph, Phillis Levin, Molly Peacock and Barry Wallenstein read the manuscript for *Now And Then: Selected Longer Poems* and provided valuable input and considerable encouragement; I want to thank them publicly. I also wish to express my appreciation to Joan Adelson Dwyer for her assistance in helping to put all of the pieces together and to both David and Diane Biesel for their friendship and their faith in my verse. And, of course, without my wife, Freda, all things would be thoroughly diminished, including the words and lines that follow within the accompanying pages.

⌣⌣⌣

Author Comments

The verse in *Now And Then: Selected Longer Poems* spans more than forty years. For good reason, this collection of long poems constitutes more than just a series of favored poetry pieces, composed in a preferred genre; rather, the volume also charts a journey to places and history into which I fell, gravitated or wandered and then chose to call my own. This characterization should not be surprising, of course, for there is a literary premise, I believe to be true, that a poet's authentic autobiography lies in the corpus of verse she or he has written. And, doubly telling, longer poems, modulated from those singular moments associated with shorter poems, should more naturally divulge major and minor secrets, refuges, harmonies, traditions and suspicions.

Why craft a volume of selected poems at all—beyond the simple advantage of having one's work readily in a handy venue? It's a decent question, but the presentation of selected poems, as an artistic juncture, refines a process— that is, it can alter conventional perspective whenever verse is arranged in a thematic, chronological, or other representational order of composition, so that an emergence of a pattern or several patterns occurs in which individual poems, in the context of an oeuvre, can be further examined. Perhaps, at the end, the exercise may beget special effect by way of a sojourn through a rephased mosaic.

In assembling a selection of longer poems written over the years, an obvious question comes to mind: What defensible criteria should be enlisted for choosing the poems to be part of this volume? What poetry should be excluded and on what basis? As I considered possible answers, I felt uncomfortable picking a poem for inclusion I didn't particularly like anymore or one whose sentiments or structure may have become somewhat foreign to me. Thus, there are longer poems I determined to leave out of this collection.

A necessary decision for *Now And Then: Selected Longer Poems* involved the ordering of the poems. Needless to say, an assortment of available approaches came to mind, ranging from thematic to eclectic; however, though revision can adjust the final completion dates for individual pieces, staying as close as possible to original composition dates for poetry to be contained in the volume and sequencing the poems in a logical panorama from the oldest to the latest should, I think, prove the most sensible way to order the verse.

In 2006, my selected shorter poems appeared in *St. Paul's Chapel & Selected Shorter Poems*. The assignment of poems passing my favorites' test, previously noted, to one or the other volume was based on a poem's length without a specific page requirement—a purely arbitrary standard on my part, to be sure; still, I don't think a reader will quibble too much with the approach. A couple of poems placed in the selected shorter poems could have arguably been part of this longer poem collection, but I ultimately decided they should be left well enough alone where they now reside.

The verse in *Now And Then: Selected Longer Poems* was written over several decades as discrete pieces without much thought given to the possibility that they would, at some point in the future, be brought together into one volume. Since the works were composed and revised over several decades under disparate conditions and, no doubt, under somewhat differing personal views, the ability to discover involute commonality among them may be a bit thorny. The poems have simply become what they are, and I see little purpose in my trying to exegete them into any palpable uniformity.

In *The Mixer; Pater, Magnificus: Story of Pug;* and *For Conduct And Innocents*, the reader will encounter "elastic rhyme," which I have used repeatedly for both short and long poems. In fact, for a good part of my writing life, I've "fiddled" with the application of elastic rhyme, which I began in my twenties to design and employ from time to time. As a result of the attention given to this model in several of these pieces, a short summary is set forth here. Elastic rhyme supplies flexibility while adhering to form but, at the same time, curbing monotonous, singsongy impacts that repel most of today's poetry audience. Thanks to its protean quality, the arrangement can be helpful in giving more vibrancy to prose poetry, which enjoys considerable, contemporary currency. An example explains best. Rhyme develops in *For Conduct And Innocents* between two consecutive lines (akin to more classic structures), each of which normally aggregates about ten words to be applicable, but the point at which the rhyme actually comes to pass will vary—thus, the term, elastic rhyme, which can strike as either a feminine or masculine construct—maybe, even a variant. As the form is practiced most often in *For Conduct And Innocents*, a poet benefits from the facility of having a key word in the first part of every other line rhyme with one of the last words in each succeeding line; it should be noted, however, I have, from time to time, withheld use of elastic rhyme in this piece for a few lines that otherwise qualify—in those instances which I thought benefit the poem. Variations to the pattern in *For Conduct And Innocents* are present for *The Mixer* and *Pater, Magnificus: Story of Pug*. Form that supplies greater discretion over the placement of rhyming words can aid a poem's diversity and richness. The approach is a reasonable extension of past poetic adaptations. For instance, as illustrated by the Psalms, the ancient Hebrew found three and two stress lines attractive; yet, for many generations now, English and American readers have desired a much longer line with increased variety. Elastic rhyme builds on the expansion and liberalization of line use without rejecting form altogether.

In *Exile* and *Martin*, the reader will observe that quatrains have been woven into longer poems. Although quatrains tend to be freestanding—at least in most conventional compositions, they can serve as a transition or interlude between sections within a longer poem and become additive to a poem's message and weight. Besides, quatrains are frequently fun to write and read.

The Civil Rights Movement shaped the attitude for many of us who grew up white in the American South during the 1950s and 1960s. The eloquence, temper and simple power of the Movement broke down families and altered plans; children reared in a seemingly implacable persuasion were sometimes reformed into puissant contradiction and consequentially less prejudicial convictions. I hope and trust that some of this verse is infused with the spirit of the times for the reader in works, such as *The Mixer; January 12th, 1967; Meditations On Civil Rights Activists;* and *Martin*—if not also contextually in *For Conduct And Innocents,* though this poem, this drama in verse, covers a different historical period.

The attention given to long poems on my part is far from over, but it is high time to plumb, through the publication of *Now And Then: Selected Longer*

Poems, where it has led and is leading, represented by these nine pieces, which have occupied a not insignificant part of my writing career. The long verse caught seasons and events to assert itself and did not rely determinatively on abbreviated moments or episodes that have been a prevailing feature for much postmodern, American short verse. Indeed, it takes a dissimilar eye for more variegated and narrative verse, built upon more protracted and evolving motifs, themes and happenings. Since the eye isn't and shouldn't be limited to the appeal of one contour, one vista, I invite the reader into the alternate provinces of these long poems.

—J. C. J.

A word or two about clues in shadows
Tell the story of a family that left home.
It begins with a half-hewn hamlet,
Where silence intones more silence
Amid perspiring, languid breezes
In fern-cornered Monticello,
Where space affirms solitude there;
Slits alive in the rough-edged pine
Vent white vapors off a blinkless sun.
Long roles edit short subjects there.

—from "Reunited In Café Divino," published in
St. Paul's Chapel & Selected Shorter Poems;
Copyright © 2006 by J. Chester Johnson.

THE MIXER

The Mixer

Preface

For the school year, 1969–70, I returned to the South from New York City to teach at the African-American public school in Monticello, a small town of about 5,000 inhabitants then, located on the cusp of the Mississippi River Delta in southeast Arkansas—the place I had lived from about the age of five until I turned eighteen. It was the year before full racial integration of the public education system in Monticello, and I taught the sixth through the twelfth grades; for a white male of twenty-five, reared in the midst, this period of pedagogy and proximity came as a chance to find people I'd known but not found. I also entered the race for mayor. At night, over the course of the campaign, African-American men often escorted me through their parts of town. On one such night, Bobby Singer, who went by the tag of "Breeches," and I appealed our way down a street I'd never explored. At the end of the street, a house, more worn than others, was steadied on two-foot cement blocks. A child's voice from within probed the dark, "Who is it?" "'Breeches'. And I want ya'll to talk to someone." The door opened into a tired room of two double beds—the room's only furniture. A white man, about sixty, maybe less, gasped for air in the older bed; he paid us little attention. The young girl who led us inside, Gwendolyn Hughes, one of my sixth graders, stood close, and pointing to the one who suffered near us but afar, she said in a matter-of-fact monotone, "Some call him 'Bill'; others call him 'The Mixer'." Suddenly, I focused on the lighter tinge of her complexion, and my imagination billowed; not until months later, back in New York City, did it settle down. A tale of love and woe, this verse, written in a form of ten syllable lines with elastic rhyme (summarized in the Author Comments to this volume), is narrated by The Mixer's white friend. By the way, I lost the election.

While the following poem is a work of fiction, the introductory commentary, set forth above, is not and therefore calls for the advantage of pseudonyms, which have been applied to persons involved.

3

Near eve, as day barely beckons night, I
recalled past words that were kinder than most.
The mattress: Gray, lumpy and tattered; and
he lay there, lonesome ghost, muttering near
about the cold and testaments. Weak street
light had leaked through cracks in planked floors and walls.

I guess he knew the treat well (better than
anyone else 'long the way) – how to live
out a hard story, but that alone they
stayed daily redemptive for each other's
torn things. The blacks were afraid he might kill
her one day or the whites might come and burn
out all the will. Again, he looked within
death, trembling with washed-out splotches braggart
over an ashen body, blue toenails.

He'd repeat the curt name, "Jacob," again
(an unknown with a call we recognize),
as if a colleague might then pull safe days
somewhere from distance, "Jacob." And the wife
kept praying without holding caution straight,
as though she, rife with a long story for
an old view, shall now resemble panic –
Lucy had little of hope left, begging
the mechanic night wouldn't close on him.

The black friend and I – we'd awkwardly hear
and bear more stories: Some the way others
told about a bristled, sheer winter; and
in the sourness of summer, dust had owned
The Mixer, who worked with no thumb after
he jammed a toned gin one September when
a hand got caught in metal works; the years
the crops failed and the family ate dough
by candlelight, and the tears talked about
everything but food; and then those machines
came. . .pickers that could do in a half hour

what it took old routines all day to do;
no more mules lined the rows, and hand plows leaned
against the barns; everybody moved to
town, and preened farmhouses broke down a board
at a time until they were all used up
for firewood; then, money came from the mail
in a tasteless cup for doing nothing –
The Mixer didn't like that, for children
never learned the path money traveled home.

The daughter sat crystalline on the floor
across the room by her lover and hummed
so indifferently she was freeless.
Bravely unplumbed, she surmised pregnancy,
even shyly – it meant little amid
the incautious scene – just to her context.
She, fussily hid, perhaps musing how
dark the baby could be and the color
of its eyes. Sixteen and full of acid
impatience? The visitor life to be
much too long 'til she could also act free.

Younger children, several set almost
as wan as Bill, three as dark as others
on the street, knocked around in the next room,
feeling the dead mood through the wall, playing
wild so the tomb wouldn't be felt. They had
already learned on the street, as Bill said,
"If your cares grow too far from laughter, then
games instead give you relief from the cares."

A bold winter rain kept crushing the day,
and voices could be heard quickened to shacks.
Winds could still lay in open fields that night
and didn't quite make it to town, a slow
town even for southeast Arkansas, where
the land would know to rise. Just a very
hard rain outside, and blithe girls running home;

heavy shoes crunching in the wet gravel;
nobody much to roam a diversion;
whispers that everybody sensed something
unusual to be happening, so
rumors were clinging cold to the houses:
A few reports had him dead already
(we'll rush people to divinity
so that we crudely become more divine);
others had him turning for the better.
I guess it's like that on the way to death:
People find the commoner for dying
too easy to understand – they make truth
a little more confusing on their own.
He did choose a few couth souls on the street,
but he didn't have many friends through town.
Most whites wondered how he could live as blacks
lived on that hand-me-down street just beyond
the breathing sewage ditch. Other whites had
it as bad, worse even, but he had been
the odd Mixer. Story-clad blacks wondered
why whites let him live noiselessly. Yes, it's
true: A suspicious man will have few friends.

Envy admits that love was a stranger
appetite with them, that she was older
than most and didn't care much about men
before him; slowly astir, he wasn't
interested in one or any more
until they both started one fall picking
the season's crops. Love would pour a secret
for them, who didn't talk to anyone
else down a row and bent for taking fruit
or vegetables. Like a gun erupting,
occasionally his father's wilder
voice could shatter the rows, "You leave that black
woman alone. Or, for her, there will be
nothing left of you." Still, one afternoon,

as everyone left the fields and set toward
home along the jejune and dirt-dusty
road, Bill and Lucy walked off together.
Next morning, they strolled into ready rows
with something steadier that had been found.
He carried a lunch in a sugar sack.
History has it that sometime after,
they moved further back into the country
roads and went to town then only to sell
tomatoes at the auction. It's told that
his father pell-mell almost killed him on
a couple of nights 'cause of his Lucy,
but that was a long time ago during
planting, and no one really remembers.

"The bother don't sting so bad," he'd then say
to her some mornings (discovering there
enough creation from a day to serve
all creation), as they tried the calm, long
roads. "Hell, it ain't so good either, but while
the crops hold out strong, we can keep ourselves."

They called him The Mixer, especially
as babies started to come in bunches
with skin playfully a sweet, meek color
of tan; hair wrinkled of nature enough;
and blended for new grace. Did the babies
come faster after rough machines wouldn't
quit and then Bill and Lucy left the fields?
They called him The Mixer when Lucy went
to apply quicker yields from welfare. They
called him The Mixer on the sleeping street.

Slapping over the tin roof, a downpour
of rain will eat greedily on a house –
rain spell as though birth signs came out again
for the end and earth elements washed him

cleanly. Between specimen, thick mumblings
and the low calling of old and new names,
a very tired question, mindlessly made,
stood here as claims and as prayer, "Is that rain?"

The slipping dreams I could well imagine:
A worker compelled before the work; hands
outstretched sibylline to the horizon;
plants now dripping of mildew at daybreak
and lithe arms then breaking with a first sweat;
miracle fingers to awake, moving
faster than time down a row – that harvest
rhythm that is a habit forever;
beautiful, atwist fruit all in a pile,
or giant sacks of wistful cotton caught
in a wagon, as the sun's going down
and everything wrought glows either yellow
or orange; stiff mules are more steaming power
under his grip, reins snapping against hide
as a man and a mule first concur to
open up the ground; the arms once more felt
like woven wire with each sovereign muscle
cut to its svelte self, throbbing from pleasure
of work; and smelling of the mule and sweat
and fertilizer, he'd sit long before
a meal of sunset, hocks, tomato, brown
syrup, and biscuits; and the consumptive
odor of fish that drown frying reminds
him of a fugitive catch; and grateful,
all the women in the fields watch mutely,
as he sheds a shirt and hardens the back
enough, and as he turns around seeing
women see him; dirt crumbles in a hand,
sifts through devoted fingers – he shuffles
it gently and simply in drunken palms;
the tiny ten acre farm he'd rather
owned. These must have been the best dreams passing
forever further from last remembered.

Everyone here, also those braving here
braving passage, did not even whisper
now but thought of less cavalier stories
everybody thought were true. It stayed odd
about Bill: Nobody told much after
being with him, and, God knows, nobody
caught him doing much, but few people should
doubt the tales about him – bloodless coward
and understood "white trash" to lots of whites
but mean as snakes with no mercy to as
many blacks. One place it could be told he,
more than once, had just refused to fight, and
yet another spot, he'd torn the bare throats
from several grown men. Both were believed,
for fame notes that a man's reputation
depends on the people who's hearing it –
the dominions they cherish, the brute fears
to which they slavishly admit. Seldom
did the worrisome stories yet prove true,
but after the teasing voices stopped, it
didn't matter through a daze: He'd become
the stories about him, and some women
laughed at him, and others hid their children.

The five of us sat akin listening
to him breathe and struggle with fewer shaped
words or names. He became alone again,
while we escaped even on the floor and
pretended chance formed a destined purpose.
The woman, who bore Bill's children and he
sought, no longer prayed beside us – with her
head tucked between her knees, she'd not be seen.
The daughter, hands locked to a lover, let
shyness careen off blunt effects; the face
she chose didn't choose to tell more but stopped
sharply, without the next pose apparent,
on a half-dropped, allaying, benign quest.

The black man, The Mixer's fixed friend, leaned near
to my mind. From next door, he'd dreamed with Bill
of more souvenir times – when the weather
was good, how they could smell the land. This man
knew he was lucky – he had a job (with
the funeral van driving funerals),
but he had a job. "I wish I could work
regular like you, too," Bill would say now
and then on rich, quirk evenings when they would
talk just to be together. And then, there
was me, white, like quintessence of silver,
on the oldest share of the floor, mourning
a coming death. If I hadn't changed so
and this town hadn't changed, I couldn't be
here now. I realize the show as well
as cost of it, and I am ashamed by
it – that what I love is only what I
learn to love and I am allowed to love.

We met oddly the first time when I got
back home, going on ten more years ago.
A stout one, blot-balding too much for my
early twenties, I'd then heard of Bill, but
there was no reason to appreciate
him; during one uncut afternoon, I
took a wrong street where he kept digging out
the ditch that passed the home. I talked away,
as Bill searched about my unskilled style; I
guess I began to love his liking me.

A common horse philosophy will tempt
us best: Not newly abstract or gutless;
surely nothing to be taught in school; just
a very hard will to live with what you
like – what you must dislike doesn't matter.
He shared a tougher tilt, and when I'd find
myself believing him too much, much would

seem much too true. He inclined us to think,
more than once, it was people who misused
fate, which was really pretty pliant. I
wondered how a used man right off the fields
could think as he could. He only had time
remained the reply – with crops gone and no
jobs or rhyme still around, with the anger
and the system denying hope and land.

He spread, as a lot of fearful folk told,
like a disease (not the grand, cruel way
some meant): You just became more like him and
didn't try to see yourself the way you
had before, all firsthand, ever again.

It seemed he lost his head for a couple
of things: He'd talk about the constant change
of supple seasons, as though it were now
to spell the last time he'd glimpse redemption,
and for his eyes it was, I guess. "Every
winter will run at sort of a certain
plowing – comes different, treating the land
different. Now, listen, when one crop dies,
habits don't stand up the same." Maybe he
sung it right, though I kinda doubted if
anyone ever noticed. The other –
a proud, stiff craving for good food; he'd say
he'd walk a long morning for a fine meal.
Only this 'morn, I wandered the kitchen –
grousing shelves could appeal to his small laugh.

Precious things come only in great amounts
and are not often in a man's life: He
sits and counts patiently for them, but if
too patiently, they never come, and if
too impatiently, they are missed. Among
contradictions, it's just a whiff of luck.
They had loved each other, he knew that well:

His loving her a bit more probably,
though he'd never tell – you could just receive
from his recollections something willed more
tender than hers, whose at times seemed flat or
bored or tired. A long time 'fore he mentioned
Lucy – then, all at once – from a plucked, ripe
satisfaction. I was privileged, I
knew that too well. A stereotype? – I
hold tight phrases and believe he'd persuade
me to search him further for frank blessings
as he conveyed the friend that he now was.

Theirs, surely love that got better at peace.
It ever gradually grew steady
and fresh – if apiece, they would share and weren't
denied – a good deal of living slowly
together and not many fights. Of course,
the toughness – that's what clarity had taught:
The hard times with few friends and little work
and sometimes no jobs, cold nights with no glad
electricity and no perk wood to
burn out the frost, or blistering under
the tin that held all the sun, or the land
was gone forever, or the offended
garden didn't grow anymore. It was
hard being together alone with fast-
asking children and the gnats-buzz measure
nature barely gave. There, that out of hard
times came a strong love. For him, it made him
stronger. Barred, I didn't know about her.

I felt the carelessness as the first son
came home. Springtime again, it'll be two
years since he left the skeleton temper
of Chicago. I, transfixed, when he threw
the duffel bag into a quiet room
and waited to hear overdue pleasure
from someone. A sister soon cried, spinning

scrawny arms around his neck, and Lucy,
gently preserving more distant thoughts, kissed
and hugged him. He shook The Mixer's baited
hand and mine quickly and went away. It
became the late, inflated summer before
I saw him again – he pretended there
had been no early chance for us to meet.
"And so how can we bear an excuse?" Bill
swore and swallowed a large reason the son
wanted home. But, like all secrets, of course,
the secret was the one that finally
told. First time in anger, Bill grouched the rare
scamp should probably still be in jail. And
then once, a fair face, hurt by confusion,
he wondered why anyone cared to burn
down a store and what were Jews anyway.

Once taciturn, the son had been favored
more by Lucy, and then I saw he could
be arrogant: Careless comparisons
he made; and standing mean with laughs, he smiled
when we didn't like him. A sly colorness
to be blamed on nods that decorated
him noblesse, the easiest skin among
the children; for while early in school, he
pranced 'round like any peacock showing its
colors, arranging parody with such
sweet taunt, and next bragged on the gifts of white
freedom. Behaving in foreign roles and
remote voice, lying bright on a neighbor's
front steps to await attention for a
difference, he kept an audience on
himself with words that relay, impel hard
response to quiet quietness, "Black men
will always drink the worst of these places –
suffering has often been in deadly
tolerance, and there's no proof you've ever
suffered for a cause. What's the clear result

or greater reward? A more convenient
suffering? Every compromise has your
weakness and supports the certainty of
your next impure defeat. You've been waiting
around here all your life for a white man
to do a thing for us – we don't even
get a crumb from a veteran corn stick.
White men help white men, and that's it. Black men
help black men. An exit is the relief
you have. So, then, freedom's the only way
to stop pain – freedom rejects history.
Now, take the excellence of the cities,
like Chicago. We're freely building there
a black man's country – black stores, black cafes,
black nightclubs, black banks – through black money. And
the motive stays black, or shame will kill us."
A bald oak reminded me of thoughts that
occur in winter, as the arch voice no
longer assumed me at its broad complaint.
I tasted another emotion, but
I couldn't finish its size; embarrassed,
a little gut-scared, a little crazy
even, I knew in a way the promise
he meant: I didn't belong there is what
he could not dismiss, and if I didn't
belong there, then Bill didn't belong there.

Rain soon withers, as more sounds do try
the weather; elsewhere, Bill had stopped even
muttering. How damned easy it is to
die (and I reached up to test his strength) – you
make noise and fight all through your life and then
always die like any beggar. She turned
on him, she turned on him, buying the son's
grief and ice-burned predictions he made; and
the things the son hated she suspected
hated him. Bill didn't think the words would
ever end rejected. "She sure missed him

a lot, more 'an I knew," he'd say without
a wrinkle to a lip. "She chose always
to fancy about him, to build special
confines for his beliefs, always helped him
more than the others – maybe 'cause he was
the first gem, a boy, or for something else."

Just a sparkle (they droned when they called me),
a blade popped open in the sun, and death
shimmered and struck – sanctity drains from each
violent fact. Bill knelt unfree into
the sidewalk and held a torn side; a son
running toward the few railroad tracks caught last
vistas of a dreaded father beside
the bus station – with Lucy standing like
a wife of twenty-three, undried years. We
lifted Bill with fear and left a blood spot
for the stories. We carried him all three
blocks home – a blanch-hot stranger, the better
friend and me. I knew everything to know
without asking: The bus for Chicago
passed rather low and everyone stared; Bill's
wife, deserted, fiddled two tickets; I
suppose Bill strained to keep her from going.

I considered the sigh way that always
worked the same and a rough house which doubled
everyone's honesty – rain just peppered
the tin. The bubbled children hit the wall
again: Where could they go, how could they go,
and what will they balance with this moment?
The black friend slow-crawled angrily to weak
feet, looked into the last features, which now
remained of Bill: "But who matters? Yes, he'll
come back. How tomorrow, he'll bring the mail
and collect the rent, sell me bad whiskey
and try to buy my daughters. He'll cuss me
and call me just anything he wants and

break my heart and break my back. All the sure
signs of pain must hide his truth once over.
Next, we'll meet the other Bill tho, prissin'
down the street, waving to everybody
and asking how the morning is, letting
our children go by. Luckily, for certain,
everybody'll wave back and tell him
the morning's just fine and we're gonna get
even better, top of the rim. Yes, I
see him coming right up to me, and we'll
sit upon the porch and talk as we used
to. Far down the road, he'll steal some laughing
now. Great God, I see him laughing now. Pain,
like an oak, cannot grow to the sky." I
breathed richly on soft rain at the screen door,
but the chill of death rattled me. Soon, land
will blossom out all over again; men
will feel the sun and eat blueberries in
a fertile shade. Someone else shall have shone
on Lucy. The Mixer brought tomorrow
but left today older and us alone.

JANUARY 12ᵀᴴ, 1967

January 12th, 1967

And so it was once said, "A city's the land
Disturbed – half danger, half hunger." The turnpike,
Auxiliary advent along the bounds of the City,
Highway of an empire, empowers tankers
Taming oil and jitneys saving much and many, as
Limousines move a rare kind of man-giant, so it seems,
And, at call, carriers of a lesser means
Collect younger souls to invade the City.

A quest and adventures once more from hushed home,
That smaller town of dreams, where boys of twenty
Take leave and uncover domains, merely undisclosed.
A fierce muscle joining the back and neck again
Twitches and pleads for renewal: I've come 1200
Miles without sleep. In America, we learn, is rest
So trifling – but the truth of the belief may yet be
Our strength. A broadcast of news does elude, though I tune
Each clarity to dissolve the gnarled absence of sleep;
Eyes too ready to back down from constant aim,
And a body holds too heavy; I stick harder to
Implacable plastic. At home, Mother –
A laugh hanging out on the words – will joke, "You
Look like death in a new white suit." One foot
Endures on the willing speed pedal,
While hours have diffused since the last meal; for sake
Of suggestion, my stomach wrinkles once or twice
Too mindfully; it can wait a little longer.

Even if I do not prefer them, friends'll defer
And ask each other when I'll arrive, but are friends,
So immediate to the City, friends at all?
To wander is to redeem an American,
So that minor thoughts of lonely perception
Will absolve; or, revived by contradictions, maybe
We're just inspired by someone else's loneliness?

Slick, white, red and quite evasive, Little Car was
Bought to roam – a good immunity to classic

Myopia. Mostly, I've tried freedom for
Short trips and abortive long ones; always to steer
A careful course cursively home; to regain better
Reasons to return than to stalk daily
This country – to ingest its feelings and
Devote myself to it, to love it better, to
Gather it by spending my youth with it longingly.

In soporific effects and a bit acrid, too,
But here I am: Horns blaring, the sound of metal
Cascading. Motors deepen. Some drivers gone daft, base.
Grand queues of clamorous traffic; who are they?
I was no witness to humans and machines mingling
In theoretical compatibility
And noisy enlightenment; certainly, I hadn't
Observed these accords, one day into years,
By inorganic choices to propagate.
Autos squashed in shoulders: Wheelless cars, russet-rusted
Axles. Warped, bowed and cleaved hoods. Someone drove a plan
Nowhere. Two automobiles, junked carcasses,
Lean on each other. Imagine new machines then
On some high venture will, on some tomorrow,
Also be hanging stripped and condemned.

Induced toward New York, objects and more skew
For space. Posters. We jam our brakes and adapt
To escape, swiping property at every chance.
To honk as though we've lost conscience; if I drove
This way through Arkansas, I'd surely be
Arrested without notice. A restive truck jerks
Onto my side, and I blow him out of the path
With horn braying. The press of moiled fatigue
Affects a selected scheme. It's surely not
Sequential to want something as much as I do,
Engaging a desire, to be even
As unconstructed as I am. Out of murky
Progress and alone in pathological sounds,
I'd wish to wander home: Monticello

Of an unfallen afternoon with neither rough
Edge as motive nor fast pace as peace.

To fail a view I radicalized. But
I can't, magnifying the country and
Verifying so much of its promise
Against its pursuit, live from hand to mouth.

And somewhere in the midst of this alternative,
The City's mine, and Victor and Mary-Helen
Shall strain for their ideas to work here. Proud, yet
Young exiles from our past, they will, of course, wish to
Skulk in iconic times and places but will laze
Over each home-logged script recited. They dote on the
Forsaken town (Victor – erstwhile professor there at
The local college), like those who could pass on
Its future; they remember in laughs its adamant
And let their imprimatur be unfair
And agree how they embarrass the town
Or how it could embarrass them – Monticello,
Still adding to varied legends. Anyway, it
Will spoil you once, and you never recover.

A dented sign at the filling station does presage
Things fading, as I waste miracle and constricted
Gasoline by jabbing at others and at
Collective mission. Metal scraps of no worth
And minor shards of glass gravel the driveway. Pumps
Smeared with oil. From a feckless try at a shave,
With eyes of the gas attendant bloodshot-straight,
A breath imbues with cigar trace and antiseptic;
A gorbellied swell overhangs a belt, the spot
To stuff a towel; hands, beefy and feral. When
He clears the windshield, rubber that sewed such tense
Glass crackles. "Today's a tester," and he grins through
A reward of silence. "The way they're showing out,
Something's gonna climb on those bastards, for sure." The
Towel's also available for anger. "You know who.

Not for a Goddamn thing they lie around. And
The government just excuses them. But that's over
If they keep this crap going. Let'em riot –
So, get us mad enough." Satisfaction
Running so deep he couldn't have heard another voice,
But hate is out on his body. And he'd
Tear into me if I gave him only a crack.

The aptitude of cities burning –
The blocks I wend by compile covens of common
Failure, and the bearers of multiple scars here
Know hardly an option to trouble waits.
Either Little Car grows more willful or I
Grow more doubtful. All directions look to converge
Into the same enclave; so, I drive the nearest street –
I'm following an uncertain instinct that I
Find to be a suspension of choice and, yet,
Sense I am blindly leading myself the right way.
The City confines its better self, while I
Shake my head to save the eyes from the weight
Of no near sleep: Languor does deny
Courage. In a far and more native place,
Dense pines would persuade over us during
Any walk through timber that will, swollen
Gray in the cold, echo to tender sounds,
Laving over unmuffled and temperate ground.

Voices, warnings dug deep inside walled streets; homes stacked
On homes; trucks now gorged; roaring drivers, well-tried
Between freedom and duress. And the grind, mastication
Of garbage. All the alarms, motors and horns. And
Thick heights, part of sweep and volume, reign. Deviation,
The logic, the recourse compress – into
Popular guts of the City. Detached
From contact and custom: Not seeing others,
But fearing their numbers; not even presuming
Composition, but another flat,

Turgid form; so, as drama tries its lesson,
I console myself in attitude or access.

He, gaunt and oddly sweating through a sweat-browned
Jersey inside some dirt-splayed window; boys with
Hair riding long and ludic; foreign language at
A corner, where shouts discount words and phrase.
Artificial lights borrow from day with the sun
Betrayed by architecture; the darkness does not live well
Here among effulgent parts, with pain going where there's
No shine. Girls wait alone, the well-dressed wave
Fast for a taxi to take them away, couples
Glare off and talk into themselves. Sure, one
Could drive forever eastward along a crosstown
Channel, when short distance amplifies a siren, once
South in the island – a cold, demented plan,
Rising further into a louder, nearer,
More desperate cause; sirens bedeviling; sirens screaming
Revenge; they're raging for protection. Four
Police cars cry through us and swerve a knot
Of neural traffic, while our perspective follows
As far as it can. Red flashes blinking out
Of sight. Police head north somewhere I've never been
And only a wrested curiosity shall
Ever launch me. I delay, daring so much
Divergence; anticipating aversion
Erupts into aversion. If, having
A certain notion though no one listens, do
You jerk and demand someone to hear? For,
After all is finally burned and everyone's lost
Most somehow think should be, the ones left are still
Each other's final and urgent consolation.

Gardens with new hedgerows and old flowers can split
An avenue, and shops, barely comfortable
In clenched space, winsomely run along the thoroughfares.
Manikins hang naked, awkwardly permanent.

Wide temperaments, too well kept. Manicured promenades
Look manicured. Wrought iron fences, whisked with carved
Motifs, handsome as well as easy. I distrust
The uncomfortable lingerer, who'll play servile
To smile at tough wives for a tip. Another
Inefficient beggar, drunk in a corner, leans
To ask for any passing coin and falls into
A hole to sleep the dust off recall. An abiding
Thought remains so normal it's now vague: Here,
The City, panorama of omission.

Plainly claimed by impervious streets,
Consumptive, pitiless streets, I gaze at symbols
Becoming more human, which yet regard
My solitude as an imputed weakness.
I resemble more specter, a solemn
Foreigner, hired to fully construe
Indigenous appetite. Eyes contracting
In undiffused light, a distended nerve, no sleep;
A finger meekly tapping whenever I think
Of the ambience of night, of cabals of display.
Different places deal different times.

Such neon testimony. 24-hour
Parking. A flagellated Little Car. Cities
Weren't inseminated for cars – that's the truth.
A curb jutting at an exposed tire bumps
Constant dizziness. The lot is empty.
A lazy dog chews a hat by a disabled
Fence. Anyone here? I switch off the motor;
Cantankerously, Little Car snatches and stalls;
The details of the trip deposited amid
A machine – New York City invitation.
Vacant to contours of direction or reprise,
I feel the chill of not knowing occupy my neck.
Victor had lectured, "No, it's easiest first to
Call from Grand Central." The street conforms to
The remnants of fatigue with emptily

Riven boxes, plentiful in crashed-out windows;
Tart garbage falling over gutters. Sounds
More sequestered, almost mean – I don't expect
Every unplumbed noise as it snaps. The withered sun
Sneaks out of walls, over pious buildings,
Beyond height. Event fallen, systems blast.

By regular shags of wood and cracks of brick,
I recover to the warm fragility
Of a bar – its caustic odor of cloth-rot
Being too human. Is descent always
Resolved into remote subtraction? Machinists,
Steadily unraveling the day's protean
Narrative, increase the value of a joke by
Increasing the noise. Not yet to Grand Central, still I'll
Try it here, a test, as I ask the peripatetic
Bartender for a phone book, but the names openly hide.
So, I lapse, order a beer, and will blend.
Workers mumble about a site: How some do
Or don't do their jobs; rivets being misplaced,
And drilling's off schedule; lines followed perfectly –
The veterans' task; new men, fucking up things
Again, perform as though they'd never seen
A fine piece of equipment. In a few years,
Nothing'll get built. Grease rests like an ancient sore on
A lean cheek as one more spent then amply
Exercises the right to rant on yet another
Travail: What's happening there? How many police,
Firemen or thugs killed, injured? A small fellow
With husk for a voice – he doesn't dread discord – blurts,
"It should be cleaned out. Take'em and not let'em back
Until they're checked. Police'd know who to arrest
Next time." One drunk, no longer sunk deep in sleep,
Sways on an uncertain balance and murmurs, "Is
That kinda stupid? To kill a dog to get at
His fleas?" A devoted stranger, sufficient in
Separation and confidence, then delivers

A token outrage, "Shut up, 'ya old son of a bitch,
What do you know?" Loud talk wanders off like a stray child.

"How do I get to Grand Central?" I invoke a kind
Of mercy from the muscle-faced black man, sitting
At ease alone. He must perfectly spin a
Perfectly new quarter. "Just up the Avenue."
"How far?" "42nd Street." Now, coarse but pointed,
He still imparts more than I think he will: "Stay on
The Bowery 'til it's Third Avenue. Straight 'til
You hit 42nd Street. Then ask someone." "Can
I walk there?" "God yes." Extra words rub harder
From disinterest? He turns slowly to wind up
An impact and seems to guide a cold, carved stare into
The pit of my naivete. Concluding in
Independent indolence, I stop the
Experiment, "I'm a stranger to all
Of the City." For release from complex
Completion of an opinion, I gulp the friendly
Beer. Starchy and too warm. Not deliberate
Nor wary, not rivalrous, he scales me again.
I say, "And the City was never home." Then,
A relaxed mouth, he chuckles, "I wouldn't have known."
"Arkansas." "I'm from South Carolina, myself.
Naw, not really. Just born there. We moved here after
That." Contrasts define similarities the way
A strong silence can define memorable discourse.
He continues the private language of our swift
Agreement. "You see those hardhats, sitting in
The booth together? They come here every night.
They're always griping, giving shit to drunks, too.
Soon, if it ain't about hippies, it's blacks,
And if it ain't them, it's politicians
Or bankers, the drinks got too Goddamn much water
In 'em, or this place stinks to high heaven. I don't
Like hippies, and politicians ain't worth nothin',
But you don't have to keep jawing over 'em. Did
You hear that crap about everything falling down

When they're gone? I work 'cross the street from 'em, and
The bunch sits around, bullshitting all day, and yells
At striplings not taking up the slack for 'em –
Then raises hell if the kids don't quite get what's asked
Or can't complete it in the amount of time given.
Ain't no changing a leech from being a leech."

"That's not fair." While I don't sound committed enough,
He doesn't need me, too. "You Goddamn right it's not.
Sure, kids are loafers, but they'd work if they knew
The program. It's a matter of trusting 'em."
He'd focus by pressing on a moustache. The story
He tells he carries low, as though, somehow,
The set of rude antagonists could hear.
I pay and nod the kind of notional nod to
A friend that says I want to find him again. No.

Rich darkness had inhaled parts of the City, as
We had played with our identities. Heels leave no sound.
Cities: To meet strangers should you rise to
Receive someone, who, in turn, shall progress
Directly to multiplication, magnifying
A particular. I stir with strangers I can't
Omit – the completions we should have if
The selection to decide us were more fixed.
A clattering of metal then frames a moment
When, as if closing curtains, a hasty driver,
Once locking a warehouse, spreads a fence and ties
The front with giant chains to build safety for
A tenebrous night. Such a slant. Not fragmented,
Not imagined. But a fitting defense?
The lock on the chain snaps shut. Gutters, indeed
Replete with a day's worth – half wrappers, torn
And wadded; newspapers; a letter from
An Uncle Nicos on abandoned paper. Ripped
Bricks lie undisturbed in the street, and slivers
Of glass pepper the pavement; naked bottles,
Thrown at the reft sidewalk, have unrelenting

Lids tightly wound – a few buoyant necks also
Persevere. Where ash-pale stores call for paint, strokes
Now scribbled on space with names that don't mean
A thing; and to be extruded for an instant,
The artist had primely crafted a signature.
Two drunks asleep in a store mouth; one's stuporous,
Not asleep. Prepared eyes impelled; blood's caked
A swollen socket; scratches, beginning
To scab, precede a sample cheek and chin.
Why guarded silence pleads for innocence?
Hair lodged with sudden clots of dirt and glass;
And while a scent of severe clothes, toes jut out
A right shoe – the left, a solitary
Mismatch. Pants rest oversized; two pair to
Degrade the shivering; holes to a leg,
Despotic holes for wind's anger. I deflect
The peculiarities when knuckles tap
My fingers -- Persistence, glaring, asks,
"You got a quarter for food?" An unfortunant
Demands the best of the worst of us. How
To deny charity? But he's begging,
"I haven't eaten for a day. Can you help me?
I don't get much from luck. How about sparing
A little loose change?" Every step he's practically
Outwearing me; muscatel, a stiff vapor
From pores; and the visage, dim with results –
When defeat steadily seeks something tender.
For yes. And I hurry to forget and leave him
Measuring over special uses
Of a quarter. Having then been bitten by wanton
Disintegration, I uncover, at a protective
Corner, wilder-haired students, who snigger all by
And prompt mutual trust through mutual defection.

Store traits, smirched arrays in ruin with aimless bottles
Thrown at darkness. Bitter faces, offended faces,
Together, are helpless faces, searching help so
Badly they're occluded; faces enlarged by disorder,

Faces carved alike. Police sirens howl the next
Hunt, still a few blocks away. North again. Over
The ascent of segregated alarms,
A stick of a boy, pale and thin as bones,
Leans aberrantly from a narrow, second-story
Window. Endlessly taut, a sweating ague,
Straining, ageless with a beard hiding an age; and, as
If sirens were only one message, he shrills, "Yes."
In mock laughs, "A rebellion now? No waiting?
Ingrates, you've had your day. Fascists, again rotten
To the core. You're grinding our chances into
Nothing and sorrow. Do you hear me? You've controlled
All this too long." Veins twist sinuously like a rope
At a weakened throat. Oddly, this time: "Do you
Hate me?" The shallow stare deepened into quandary. Then,
A girl, arranged from subdued scrutiny,
Reaches for rigid arms and, sotto voce, whispers,
"John, they'll arrest you. You know that, don't you? They will."
Drugged with classical madness and, also, to desert
Deftly any confines of pose, he withdraws
Abruptly from the window. As though only a vague
Idea had been tried and dismissed, he disappears.
The girl, eerily expansive in freezing air,
Slowly, mechanically shuts the obedient
Window, and she dispassionately then subsides.

The nerves cry selfishly in realness of stone.
And the creed: No one safely infers innocence from
Disillusion. Slipping on a short gradient,
I'm weakened to consider a fast break from here –
Not from young melodramatists, nestled
Clique, hiding within folds of a sack
Of a building – lonely minors, learning to speak
Loudly without courage or texture. Where can
They sleep so defended, if they cannot endow
Each other? Influence, most mildly left after
Everyone's taken parts of you, isn't much:
Enough to love another, drink, for a walk a day?

The City recovers in lights, relaxes where
Running, branding streets meet in a farrago of too
Many directions. As if staged, a woman struts,
Swinging a vivid purse, and men joke about
Jokes I can't hear and turn in sparkling bars. The streets,
Agape and enduring, ask for hope again.

Laughing gross names and laughing nicknames but laughing,
Children beat tennis balls between vans and trucks in
Distracted streets; cussed, yelling, rebelling, children
Cuss in return, nearly damned when freedom's glimpsed – a traffic
Light, effusive green. Rankling, incurring dirt, they fly
An avenue, press sweat-frosted faces against
Mirrorless glass, mock interiors, and know
Everything to happen and scatter before it does.
Flapping in white, a druggist howls from a secure place,
"You don't live around here. And don't you try to come back –
Stealing my best books." Incrimination invites
A change in plans for the runaways, escapees, who flit
Toward open spots, as though all were guilty.

The City will regularly dispense its people
And the people's other world. Crowds breed and dissolve
Into victorious rivers of humanity.
We're swept, yielded and quixotic, betting gladly
On ourselves against any interdiction; we're
Subduing all laws and snaking through
Erratic car lines. Traffic hardly bothers a herd,
For the moment's clamoring, dangerous as malady.
We cannot even imagine the persuaded
Sentiment of our gaze. While true speed's only
Used in extremes and emergencies, the City
Heralds an emergency for all to declare.
If the policeman in coveted shoes shall advance
A formula for abetting speed, we trust he'll have
The fun he thinks he will. Nothing succeeds within
The public storm. Throbbing circles of all, dumbed to
Staring at the indefinite. Pendulous, the addled

Edge, promoting a better view, rustles at random.
Firetrucks and sentinels quite physically
Separate vulnerable space. And moans
Seep the crowd. Rumors, not so slowly. Explosive threat
Or canard? Amid the unhurried search, hot boys roam
The setting. Promptly, everyone's bitter – mad
At officialdom, milieu, themselves, me. . .intumesce.
Revolts still erupting somewhere, the gossip
Now passes with a message: "Take the police
From ghettos, and the risk will end." We wander
Absently through chance and other traps. "If
The police aren't now removed entirely from
The riots, new trouble will soon be running."
During the time a drama prevails over the crowd,
Fear of the unknown is worse than fear of the City.

A preacher in much regalia – collar and surplice –
Inveighs from a pair of tottering stools to
Gathered expectants at a mostly restless and handy
Corner, "God will have His truth. If this should be
Expiation, He's coming to find us in our noise
And in our blindness. We've heard His voice exclaimed in brave
Scripture. Shall we die by the hate we so freely give?"
Abruptly lifting a slim staff that steadies
A nameless flag while an evangelical glint
Protrudes, the cleric marshals more, "May God inspire
Caesar to choose, in his heart, mercy and atoning love."

To falter, as if palsied, though most will have
The nerve to believe in answers – I do not want part
Of me, the part that's exposed, to speak for
The rest of me. Who can accept any
Commotion without engorging it or not
Worry about a consensus? I'm touching
Many arms – bearing excuses as I
Add to a great number, checking myself
To see if I've just improved or fallen. . .
But an incident occupies so much broken space

And summons inference – the stuff that holds
A body together tossed about again.

It's immortal to walk through crowds that murmur
A close should a bomb disrupt and test the various
Senses named – surviving isn't an answer
For everyone. Finally, desires alone
Rouse all rumors, some that will and some that won't
Come true; finding even half-truths that stay true is
Exceptional, but ever inexorable.

We resort to ceaseless movement – thinning of a crowd;
Muscles shift as verdicts shift, and hearsay dies
With the decay of excitement. It's true: Rumors rise
When there's nothing else to do or when there's so much
No one knows a place to begin telling the truth.
From a first retreat by police, barricades,
An ambulance and mercurial taxis sift
Through a scrum; a businessman smiles at a stranger and,
With the anonymous voice he saved for strangers,
Dramatizes, "Will our tolerance keep getting stretched
Like this? We're insane to try to beat the City
At all." The stranger smiles back as a stranger
And broods at the executive's potent gait. Now,
United, immured silence. At once waiting for
Any apt sanction with everyone, more look at
Those troubled intentions on every side;
Conformed to delay, I then ride the crowd into
The stomach of the station. Mother said
A time or two, "If you're in a hurry to leave
Someplace, just find somebody who doesn't live there –
It won't take you long to find a way out."

The glaring size of the waiting room – higher
Than I bothered to suspect and so wide I turn
Both ways to understand the worship. Control
That's ever weighing, quiet recollections,

Laughs, and solicitudes ricochet hollow depths.
Moments that also swallow and calm a mind
Do not subtract me from the City and a quick
Commitment to leave. I'll search again for strengths –
Accept and apply them until they are gone.
Why's panic so often the first expression
Of no choice? Girls I'd known, so easy to listen,
Would leave us alone with times we had – I'd
Talked of our past so far we were prematurely
Lost in comparison. How obvious it is
To be superficial when you crave an answer
Or advocacy. Gradually bled
Of familiarity, we get weaker
Until we lie there in silent darkness staring
At the aspect we fear. I know the aspect I
Fear: A city, a cocky city, full of order
Going everywhere; fugitives, commanding speed,
To hurry for the drastic good of the country.

But already two lovers meet in a returned smile
And do not mumble about an interruption;
He anticipated all day the luxuries
Of her opinion. I flip from book into book;
Innominate pages then obfuscate to no
Good effect – telephone pages, intent to wreck
My poor plans. As though I were struck by insoluble
Ignorance, any conjecture impacts as a
Vision, and happiness depends on primal
And instant novelty – so that process is
Noisily apparent: "Operator, please, in
The area." And a hunt made beautiful by
The find: "Dobbs Ferry, Sir. 53 Heber." I
Will locate friends by the tilt of an accident.
"Dobbs Ferry. Dobbs Ferry." How to get there? To get
Anywhere? Will they be home? A phone's ring
Not registered? Will prospects include a theory
That shall collapse? Amid hours when slight hints must

Completely come true, doubt's too strong to be idly
Entertaining. It's a matter of time and
Presence whether friends can answer a wish.

Someone invisibly disturbs several finished
Cigarette butts and barely gathers a nod
At the acceleration of a crowd. The ticket
Line's for impatient aches – there's no wit to dissuade
The routine. Stalked by clumsy bags and instruments,
Commuters and distance travelers, the rich and
Penny-counters, four handsome students and a fat,
Unscrubbed sort – all defended by miscellany –
Compete for angles and rewards. Mostly,
They fidget and don't quite ask a question, while glares
Perform the reproof of an agent, who slowly counts
Light change or lengthy tickets and who replies spryly
Only if questions can be glibly answered elsewhere.
It takes a long time to learn the knack
Of acting alone, and standing in line
Is forever. A squatty, scar-nosed man talks for
The febrile rest of impatience, "Can't you hurry up,
Up there?" The bald-headed clerk in the ticket cage
Sweats terribly, even among sneaking cold drafts,
And bemoanfully misses the ruthful and foreign
Slant of my glance, so I slur, "Dobbs Ferry."
He spouts an unconscious, "Gate 3." Many
To protract a linear course cancel
Each other's path, and many, hustling to beat
The rush, are actually causing it. Tours, cameras,
Watches, cars, things advertise collective cures;
And brighter-than-live colors liquefy
The places they want us to go. Stock prices
And aseptic tickered reports, besides. Newspaper
Stands, fruit grottos by the gross. Grand Central
Station. Should a more precise voice then lean
To censure one vague and faulty sign, crowds, taking
A cue from the side, could turn on a stranger in
A second if he says something they've never heard.

Across the station, odd collections manage
The odd source of recollections; novel
Features intrude on a careful synthesis. Gate 3. . .
Comfortable rejoinders descend above
The tracks' steam and dim composition, as
The physique of the train exhibits Homeric
Symbols and aptitude; a broken burst, miasmic
Mist can still subsume one more favorite recall's
Persistent odor, which, more than any image,
Inflates a pause forgotten; for visions outline
A return, while a smell opens the buried event.
Steam boils tenderly in sight many times, as I
Wait for a hoist to adventures of a next step.
The wilderness of the new world then delightful –
I was four, maybe five, round and awkward like
A new assumption; I'm holding for dear life to
Hattie, another famous and mostly obliging
Mother of my mother. She'd lift me as she'd lift a
Light cloth, as I entertained myself by supposing trips
Infinite, but they were mere brief connections from one
Part of a family to another – all favors
And gifts to travel, replete with fun and style
And delicious characters. Though trains aren't quite
The use they once were, trains had been heroes in her life;
When she started dying off, they did, too; as
A function of the same recurring affection,
My heroes will cheerfully die whenever I do.

For a settled moment, to focus solely
On minor fragments, terse comparisons in
The strange company of empty coaches
On my implacable march to a smoking car.
While fumes irritate the head and the throat's racked,
A habit feeds a numb pleasure – I crave deflection
To depress a suspended modern age. The seats
Bear scars: Preponderant sitting, leather cracked,
Knife hacks; skin wrinkles against wrinkles, creased
For years. As soon as varying strides of

The train relax all leaden consequences,
I can conjure prospects for the future –
I'm young. I do not want to forget, just note
A city I'd never seen and melt awhile.
Two men, who promote themselves through ritual clothes
And the connotative material they read,
Agree a certain stock's weak and a bank wants more lease
Accommodations. Then, abruptness is exchanged
For stilted ease, and the two barters expertly fold
Always serious newspapers and mark
A set of gunshot holes, carried in the train window;
Deliberate rents in turbid glass match
The magnitude of a slight thumb. "It's just more
Dangerous each trip. A friend of Joe Rutledge
Got shot a week ago, and, so far, they don't have
Anybody. It's no secret – faceless boys in
Indistinguishable windows are firing on
These trains at will. Adding that rebellion out there
Today, the risks should keep us off these trains now
Or any time. We're on display at the worst points."
The mated sympathizer swallows, rolling, wrenching
The newspaper tighter than it should yield, and
Frees part of embedded anger, "It's a zoo. Meat's
Thrown anywhere around here, and I'll be Goddamn
If half the City doesn't leap on it."
Something loud quivers on his lips. "Hell, wars
Were extinct, we thought – then, symptoms had to follow
Us home. And, on the street, my God, I used to walk
Pleasantly to lunch and uncover a few friends
On the way. Now, I step out of the building right
Into the frenetic Olympics. What can
A sane man do? I try to get along, really,
But I'm told to hire so-and-so to keep
Someone off somebody's back, and I finally conclude
The hire can't satisfy the job. So, I employ
A surprise who happens to walk off the street for
A change of scenery, and he is worse. Then,
The state employment service delivers one

Of its drudges, and, I'll be God damn, we still
Make money." Vengeance disguised as logic is
As merciless as arrant vengeance. We abandon
The obtuse, underground arteries for scenes
So firm that rapid visages rebound undiffused
Off sullied glass. Emerging, repetitious
Buildings and contours of poles effortlessly notch
The passive distance we reduce. And though it has
Neither voice nor opinion, we find land working.

A common hue settles conclusively on
Remains and new construction; uncolored shirts hang
As empty torsos from fire escapes; and a torn
Off shutter. Black and near-black boys pee in wintry street
Water and try to provoke fireplugs to lave away
Presumptive grime. An impassive woman, who was
Once guaranteed a singular arrival, stands
At a kitchen. They came on faith. The exodus
Of blacks from a guilt-wearied South seduced the City
Into those costly dangers of the self-righteous –
A city's ambition, sealed in its ghettos.
More souls displaced here from among placid, quixotic
Towns and lands of the borne Southern; more countless
Multitudes, retained slavish behind austere
Windows, inspire a language, a propagation
Of detachment. Outside this unsafe, fissured
Glass, smoke drifts by the slow train: Not raging, mostly
Coiling like a corpulent pile of cloth on fire;
A pall, burning clumsily, thinner than wood ablaze –
Trailed by dense smoldering of blunt rubber, mixed
Combatively with gas and defiant metal.
The circulating cast of a kindled cloud
Distends behind a city; bland structures
Erected old. "But it seems very cold out
There, doesn't it?" The priest's haunting, elastic voice
Fosters a bribe preachers often enact
With grit, as if they would, by acts of intrigue, include me
Among an elite. "Of course, the riots are

Just beginning." "Burn it down?" My mind crunches on
My own complete question, but he answers promptly
With a smile, "'Cause they do it together. 'Cause they
Can do something together. Still, they're not killing
Any of the Other. They're mainly killing their own."
Comfortably wrapped in added solitude,
He prefers to continue singly with more
Private gist, "There were those who cared, who cared so
Much, while they saw the first killing at night long
Before – sequestered, illegitimate –
When, with everyone else then conspiring
And conflating, together stealing, buying
And pretending, calling anyone's confusion
Laziness. Yes, there were some who knew, but they were
Very silent and dismayed." Is peace taught boldly
Like propaganda? Injected like medicine?
Using tools of power and deforming
The message? Like a fast slap, he accosts,
Hinting condemnation can instead inspire
A limited, whist voice, "What are you going to
Do about it?" Sanctimony hardly ever
Intends a response. He then evades his own
Askew game, "This is my stop." And even
More, he gladly snaps a flippant, "Good-bye."

The tracks the train rides lie down bare, gray like small
And fallen oak trees. Smoke doesn't curl now but floats
Ominously, grasping on a river to
Richer towns. And as we pretend a mad,
Blindless sniper merely mocks and dissembles somewhere
And will excuse the best of us, he'll greet a train,
Dealing torment to his city in garbage-soaked
Ghettos sleep can ruin more, for sleep has him
Dream. As thoughts can rave, I imagine seditious
Clarity behind dismissed windows. Scatheless,
With charity anesthetized, voyagers
Read on, reflect on justifiable blindness,
While fires burn aloud nearby, mysteriously

Burning in resentment – dull coldness, dense rage,
Both present in a profound nature of loss. Shutting
My eyes to calm them down, I suspend hurried
Editorials; but amid a lair,
Old sayings pop; and old sayings pop in
Rhetoric, "For all those people with no
Value in their certainty will have no meaning
In their pity." Can we harbor hushed declarations
Serenely, hiding a private remorse?

Although they prefer something else to custom, riders
Surrender neatly to implied next steps.
What beast, if a beast, craves those who once slip
In death-sleepy eyes to waiting cars, waiting coarse,
Authorized? Even illumination contains
Approval by darkness, impounding the mouth of night.
Fireplaces glow toward the tracks. Dobbs Ferry. A town's
Name is a story, too; first trips across a river
Two hundred years ago rise to a crystal-steel
Freeway, leading people by restive progress now.
Modernity heaves taller than mud and stronger than
The erstwhile enervated siderails of a floating
Bridge. And anybody can get anywhere through
A simple power of need. By now, the last
Ferry captain's dead; no one remembers the red
Hat, donned for authority, nor progenitors
Buried but still busy here. A grandniece, now a waitress?
A grandson's a druggist in Omaha, drilling
For gas, plywooding in Oregon? If, by chance,
Convention can forecast description of style, the town
Suffered too much age from constancy and manners.
Shaping the past for a better future, building
The young to excuse and commit to the old,
The town superiors composed a fable, and each
Generation mimes an inorganic version.
For blocks, houses do not even alter their
Equivalent complexion, where all nightly
Evidence of near-criminal nature is then

Cited on notable porches – with muted lamps
Balanced in each window's performance, further
Washed by linen curtains. Somewhere, within the fashion
Of a family crime inside the abundant rights
Of anonymous gates, a ritual will have
Persuaded the players to continue presumption
And marry their own and have their own kind. I've seen
It: Gathering at a threat when closing is first
Complete, they will never ask anything again
For which they do not already know the answer.
Born to evasion, they preserve servility. . .
But that's not enough. So obvious a submission
Is even tolerable? Protecting each other
For themselves? Most players collectively deny
Commonality, but a few witness too late
They're servants to the idolatry they devise.
They discard reforms; they're the institution,
And they lose a little more each time they stop
Conspiring. And as compensation, immunity
Was all they expected, and it nullified them.

Near another graceless crossing but attending
A rhapsodic hitching post by an iron gate
He might enter for home, the grizzled man openly
Luxuriates in familiar streets and well-known
Directions but shudders on his steadfast cane.
As antique clothes hardly grip the antique
Body, a patched work shirt and irascible pants
Under a limp-long coat splice at a flamboyant
Waist-rope. Not with uncertainty, he invokes lightness
To an old-age process. "Heber?" he asks himself.
"53 Heber? The Anthony manor? Yes,
I know. Not a very pleasant spot there now. Stories
Of its previous prestige have vanished. It's entirely
Empty of its harmony. The house has gotten
Dull and stale with apartments. New objects litter the grass."
"I want to find my friends." "Over the hill,
Down three blocks, a right, first house on the right." The

Last sentence blasts as literal memory from
Conviction with practice: Of paint change, scandals,
Witty fiction; of decay and healthy reasons
For a tribute; of general, unalterable
Patterns; of imperious context. Trusting in
Consecrated and unconscious anecdotes on
The part of one more homogeneous town, he,
Like a friend, had calmed my disordered urge. Not by
Declarations he applied but by the style he
Played, I anticipate the apparency –
The old man was old men I had known, and
The compulsion that prompts breathes slower;
Perhaps, he had become distinctive knowledge.

Changes? Mary-Helen will again fall quiet
At Victor's words to avoid suspicion – there's
No temper, no concession, an indefinite
Outrage; changes he'll analyze until they're flat.
How normal it is that we test by willful guile.

I retrace Victor's fakery, a comic
Incongruity: "Sex must be free and physical.
If any stranger ignites you best, why deny
The body's stimulus? Mary-Helen and I
Understand about this false morality,
And she knows I've gotta try if I encounter
A woman to travel." The modulating voice
Transparently tumbled weaker and deeper, "For
Her, the same freedom holds." As I remember
The cycle of action, there was this genteel
Woman, then available among soft
Opportunities at an exaggerated
Party; and since pundits need an exhibition,
Victor clung to her intentional allure. Now
When I had then extended my own plans
For Mary-Ellen with a little confab
To entertain directly, oblique notes of jealous
Burn were sounded; for the liberal philosopher

Had turned the conservative lover. So,
Escaping pressures of theory, Victor collected
Mary-Helen like any used coat and withdrew
From gamesmanship. Early the next morning,
Separating my attention from solid sleep
Began a silent, subtle apology – first
Duty for the progressive couple, who
Produced a titanic breakfast for appeasement.
A whip of a mouth, he's almost standard
To major themes in irregular times, "The only
Revolution – from my freedom to yours." Just as
Freedom illustrates in the particular,
Maybe he's right in the long try, "To convert and
Free someone automatically transforms
An institution." Speculator in the trade
Of Freud, mostly favoring piety
Over tolerance, he isolates love from us.
And, he, less sure than the analysis
He propounds, will nimbly cater to abstract
Power and generalized logic: "New
York's a braver place. To favor growth over
Clichés, it'll nourish invention. It'll also ask
Us to affirm honesty. And since fear's not applied
As an excuse, we can uphold our genuine
Desires." Paint peeled to dirty boards, a warped
Balcony. The urge to sleep or talk bites again,
Whenever I imagine fruitful faces
That slowly nod renewal and beckon
A ceremony of recollection. Should
Victor, Mary-Helen rise? Through a plan? Around
The house, feeling as a burglar feels out prospects,
Perplexed by the taut energy of alternatives,
I eventually stand before a door that's
A monument. Neither exploding on nor attacking
The ferreted conquest, I will slowly complete
The trip and tap: Quit, louder, quit, Louder.
"Nobody there, fellow." A voice like hell contains

Me; sloped over the high parapet above,
An overripe woman severely hangs there – a Buddha
Under a dress that fits like an increscent tent. The hair's
An unkempt hedge; scaled knuckles on the freezing rail.
"They ain't in." I'm yelling, "Where are they?" "I wish I
Knew. In the middle of the night it must have been,
They packed and deserted us." Hope crisply
Unravels once the present stops being a final
Promise. I try to stabilize whatever
Remains, but she adds more text to injury, "Yes,
I called her daddy. He's a surgeon somewhere down
South. He doesn't know either, and he won't pay
The bill. They're gone. Plain gone." What do you do if
The last wish fails? Absolutely nothing. When
A last wish spurns, any close inference
Will miss the point. It always takes a strong belief
To think clearly. The deadness goes about
Confiscating desire, energy, method.
Children play with fun amid my concentration.
What inquiring laughs briefly tormenting
Do resound. Of course, I would countervail
A city that's not just craven and brutish as
A maniac on my mind but will shoot me down
Like an unleashed dog if I'm at the wrong place at
The wrong time. I've already learned it'll quell me
When I disagree with a facile attitude,
But it'll buy me a drink or a plate of food
If I don't. So, for the sake of procession or
Silent survival, you better be a pretty
Damn good lier if you plan to break even.
Victor, who snatched people by their conjectures,
Obsessed through one idea to beat the confusion –
With Freud, to lose implied misery, even though
Philosophy can only verify, not
Nurture. "To be complete," Victor said without aplomb.
But exposed, he returned to ambiguity;
Anyone who thinks being right will save him feigns.

At least bad weather doesn't step heavily; oh,
I shake occasionally with the wind, and when I
Blow into my hands, fingertips crack into peaks.
But a pluck of a man reacquaints me with the cold
Rivet by slapping himself to beat the sting out
Of a cloth coat. All digits squeeze into stiff fists
Inside moth-eaten gloves. Punctuated by
A pair of dripping earflaps, an exhausted cap
String-ties under the florid face with harvested
And wide pockmarks. Over the vulnerable flesh,
A yellowy crust lies – long years in the cold
To produce resistance. Though a throat earns him coins,
He's paid for coarse and meager noise, struggling now. One day
Follows the same day, each year to mimic the last;
But longevity fondly notes one pleasant
Recall: He never missed a chance to work.
A new scarf to flare heroically,
The well stretched shoes smile back like a well deserved badge.
And leaning on cold's wonted pain to fight
The cold and coughing a sale, he snaps
The newspaper double on his wooden chest
And concludes, "Thank you, young man." "Riots To Get
Worse – No Rain," headlines think, surmising that
The milieu, more than any other trait,
Contributes to disorder. Just as darkness begs
For light, just as tragedy steadily begs
For humor, confusion begs for clarity
To give refuge. The mouth's open; I do not hear
A report. Tracking aimed rails, I lift myself
To more platforms for a return, which is not
A return at all but recompense for not
Confirming place. Sweet steel boxes as other
Greenhouses – luxurious cattle cars steering
A conscience home? Before families can wilt
Under shadow of a real night, they'll cozy
Toward honey-fed babies and assign uniqueness
To blunt children. Contrasted against those whining trains
Now jammed to unanimity, a few loners

Wait for the next instinctive, City-minded train.
I don't know the loners, but that's not important –
I'm one of them: Night performers and night watchmen;
A custodian who follows accidents,
Extravagant in the City. The wailing
Grand sounds of the train shall inspirit
A suicidal attraction to power. As
If daringly freed from the mute celebration
Of night's inertia, an empty train tears
Other echoes out of our passive ears.
A pregnant woman, gladly careful for
Conception, enjoys that life alone can
Imagine life. Here, assaulting motorcycles,
Rippling in mythological din and barking
Fumed earth through the darkness, are weapons in
The hands of the assaulted. Against
A contemplative language, an aggressive train gulps
The opposite track, but another lone
Locomotive agrees with our direction.
If options are the symptoms for liberty,
Then constraints must emerge as the shibboleths
For captivity. Within a newspaper
That's preaching how reality always
Overwhelms good sense: Arrests of childish
Victims and more immunity for criminals;
Looters stuffing pockets with toys and liquor;
From the apex of a gun, madly discharging
History's wrath at history's neutrality,
Miscellaneous snipers mislay several
Didactic bullets; and for the dead, encircled
With prodigal blood, aggrieved innocence
Further grieves. Death to stop an argument
Also to keep customary order intact?
Police horses, trampling closest to the loudest,
Crudely teach the unpatriotic lesson
That governments must rule by threat as well as
By law. And a tightened commissioner assures,
"The smoke will die if stronger winds don't rise."

Inside this half asleep head, a cloudy view invites
A night, defining the dark by so much partial
Incandescence – with scattered stars over naive
Skies. A tiger's across the ether, and two rabbits
Peer at each other. I see a solitary,
Giant wing without an entire bird for dignity.

A laggard, at the aisle, of jutting crossed-knees,
Of a cocked fedora, hiding cocked thoughts, delights in
The convenience of image. The passing
Of lights, evanescence, fulfills the irony
Of a faded day. Such a plump and wrinkled
Pair, still heart-bitten, chuckle for secret's sake
And forbid each other any passage to
More audible chitchat, bidden by sharper social
Conduct. These lovers, duped by love's practice:
Sagas are easier to discover
When they're disguised. Tittering whispers, made
Of these love-exacted twins: "He'll catch hell,
But he deserves it – the blustering clown. Only
Conceit can stand him when he's like that. Let
Him bitch some more. Can't you hear him, Harry?
Bad temper will fit him like comfortable clothes,
'Your work's my work, and if you don't complete it,
I'll ride your back until you're through.'" All love
Shall divide into fractions: Separate circles,
Ad hoc rites – everything love hasn't been
Keeps love whole. The other half, then, sending
A diaphanous, subdued laugh, closes the story,
"I'll bet one of the owners found the mistake first.
You recognize Jack's whipped-dog look 'cause he
Didn't know the root of all the bellowing?"
The event-twins, safest with contiguity all the more:
Breath-shared exile, one more exchange of absolving
Detail. But I must settle for happiness
I steal; and, yet, a deserted train, screeching on
Behalf of a deserted city, isn't much

Of a bargain. Other headlines divine, "Riots To
Worsen." Night on night, solitude foresees
Violence from a tyranny of hints.

For sleep confounds if I worry about sleep,
While there's neither destination nor sanctuary
Amid stasis and an unresolved trance.
Discord fully eliciting concealed
Priorities of a generation. A smoky haze
But hanging on skeletal tracks. With no reason,
All moments can turn cruel. As yet even
Ungracefully, transmogrified motives ever
Modified, contorted or contested.
A city devolving into dependent
Apostates that degrade. At last, all questionable
Choices to, of course, check the order and the ordered.

No rush. No beset calm. Nothing to affirm
Margins of danger and vindictive mood here.
The conductor – bolting, bumping, coughing, scolding –
Illustrates the athletics of primacy. In
A shrilling to jerking stop, the train shortens
Its range of deliverable power; coarsely,
Soldiers scramble for the doors – back into Grand Central.

Giant ramps echo, my deaf heels clink like metal,
And, in far corners, inexact caverns humbly
Admit to obscurity. Two teenage boys
With hair wild as grass try terrible masks to
Be crazed and then melt into silence. Escape
Leaves a void; thus, loose sounds cluster, clattering
Over dissonant tiles and settling at
The mosaic pools of my feet. More softly than mere
Shards of noise, silence gnaws in a long hall.
I recognize sample rhythms of my breathing;
I cough, I swallow and slowly apprehend
My fingers raking my palm; when I shuffle,

A clunking and swishing encourage other
Revelations. Uniquely, I jump, and several
Repressed children I astound applaud. Unfinished
Sneeze, muffled yawn, disjunct trills – characteristic
Of parts in search of conjugation – carom on
Single echoes until one breach rules.

The strayers prowl in predatory daze,
As executives savor cabal's ritual
And fraternity and as we acknowledge
How trains going anywhere go nowhere
In particular. An endless reminder
Forebodes fate: To those who prepare for suffering,
Suffering can be done without remorse.

Lights disguise time and lie about primitive sleep;
Great lights, surrounded by invasive darkness,
Will falsely convince us it's day. But I know – lack
Of sleep has no challenge left. What produces
The nearest exit to night, less known than empty,
Unyielding space? Finale of doors, bistros,
Convenience, conspicuous talents –
All are bid trite and temporary good-byes.

Night strengths blurt first a fresh birth and then a bald zest. Taxis;
Happy and unhappy voices; crass machinery
Establish apparent circumscriptions of time.
Night sounds for disenamored ease? They're part of day.
Subtle flickers and huddled bodies cramp a wall:
Seven hustlers, old men and women, who adopt
Practices of old men, rub fretted hands over
Burning newspapers and cast cards into focal piles.
One of two, feasting on gloves, shares the warmth.
Those who don't play have a favorite anyway;
A practiced grab captures the evasive pelf
Of evasive money with kings over nines. Five-card draw.

Then briefly shrinking lower for fire's last remnants,
They cuss someone more for failing than for quitting.
Should gambling gratify the risen vagrancy?
Don't they know that if they win each fast wager,
The small plate of the game carries no freedom?

Drawing a road from where I stand, objects
And I blink at each other gawkily.
Things for space momentarily hasten a switch:
They're other places, hyperboles in distance,
Remembered approximations of law and love,
Antecedent seasons and lessons, claiming
Happiness is not is but was or will be.

One woman bothers to devise her ageless pose;
A mien says she either slaps up or mops up something.
Worn is the manner that's been yelled at plenty;
Enunciation flows through her short, thick body
That, perched wart-like, wields by full measure.
With cropped hair, rumpled work shirt, crumpled bag,
She still proposes easy talk and easy notion –
Not because we're alone and, therefore, directed
To talk, nor because I know her or know she knows
Me, but because we recognize that each of us
Holds the best we are for less public moments.
Nothing can reform idealizers of silence;
For they know everything can happen, and they know
Soft ways and hard ones – how to cheat to stay safe;
How if you're weak, pride'll get to you; how to cheat
And be honest. Politically wistful stares don't
Quite persuade, and only those who believe in neither
Awe nor magic will be scared by eyes, philosophy,
Or ruse. "So, 3rd Avenue can get me near
The car." "I'm waiting on a bus to Queens myself.
If early, I watch the police patrol like
They live here, where nothing much happens. How far on 3rd?"
"Far." Thus, plagued by a foreign mode of assessment,

I rather select naivete as marker.
"It's a flimflam and bastard city, you know," she paints;
But old women cannot placate a young man's context.
Remains of a very rude beer tears the stomach.

I've now absorbed corners where lights plead liberation.
A concise woman, patently pleased with
The formal luxury of provinces women
May save like bankers or children with an only toy,
Is encouraged by a mock-scotty, which is not
Even a dog for her but an urge she's
Miniatured. When cities stir with a player's whim,
No wonder, then, dogs deign to deem us as peers.

From a period of lights, restaurants and bars
Reduce constant desire to constant prospect;
Counting boys as bashful customers, girls ignite, too.
No family or others to still the caprice,
A young sloucher being casually single.
Of homes too open to be envied and jokingly
Equating manner with felicity, language
With secrets, alien voices inherit the streets.
Sons have learned to lean like fathers, who've learned to laugh
At laughing. Down into the night I quickly touch,
Skies, more remote, posit an incomplete answer
To faithless prayers. Stars, blinking in shadows,
Retard the grosser articulation
Of bricks and recover part of freedom that's
Almost a quiet winter night in the fields, where
A starved, plangent wind is a dog, howling for nothing.

Street lamps segregating darkness – slowly, mere presence
To extrude chaos, reflecting the kinetic
Ambition of movement. Not as young as he
Should be, a bent, unbendable man reaches
A post more as a place to be than as a prop;
A beer bottle, swaying, gathers fingers of a hand.
He scratches with the fleshy ferocity

Of delinquents and shares a tin cough. Even tart
Sounds cannot keep from expounding the litany
Of absence: Bits of frozen mud under a shoe are
Snapping like twigs; hollow cans across asphalt.
People disappear, not because the night's older,
But a murky cast drifts too far, where I
Shall snatch occasional light off evading taxis
Or such illuminated guardians that scare
Away clumsy thieves. All the night propounds but
A blurred balance of individual nuance.
Cautiously included in bowels of the City,
Even normal observations are abnormal.
Preliminary sounds held in shred-bare whispers
Of the corner, up an alley, beyond a wall?
Resonant, private, atomic, vicinal, spare
Orders, impelled by insinuation;
But I don't save a bum, who, lying coatless in
Thin sheets of ice on rare weeds, whose moans tap
My bones, may learn that, among assorted
States, capitulation can also become greed.

Like rat eyes, like cats of standard condescension,
Dead eyes break from monotony and squint stunned that
I bother to contradict a night with its covert ways.
A night of accents: Part lies that demonstrate
A truth and those intuitions that never
Quite make it to an idea; escalated
Wishes as stealth. Hours ago, I passed
Here, as misshapement could get worse. Now, a dog,
Commonly starved, hunches at fence poles and sniffs for
A bitch. Distant cars, muffled by the City,
Resemble words, too far removed. Manacled stores and bars,
Bearing stoic self-preservation, stand witness
To the sovereignty of various hours
And attitudes of a day. Learning from
Architecture the techniques of those physical
Defenses against unpleasant winds, bums rely
On the ingenuity of curves and junctures.

Constitutionally rhythmic, lucky drunks, very
Drunk and drinking; a human effect talks only
With arms, asking for samples of forgiveness –
As I regard guilt a condition of solitude.
Still, trusting my doubts, I know ambiguity
Is, first, the result of mercy. Thus, all objects
Shall suggest rescue, and I gaze at
The red deterrence of a sign. Radical
Prospects enter a cold stone head; solemn
As wood, with everything and absolutely
Nothing telling me to mind the details,
I cannot modulate extremism
In the physical particular.
Hot, smooth blood riots an eye and tears me dizzy,
Busted blank against the flinty and fractured
Symmetry of a wall. Waiting hushed to be
Tempted, a cool, lean razor rests on the right side
Of my throat; cracks along the wall gouge my back – I'm
On the way to a knee and finally to concrete.
Just like rats out of a coign: "Boy, what you got?"
The mouth, steaming with spit and hair, shielding such blanch
And intemperate skin. "What do you have we want?"
The other thief, gray-flushed in shadows, has pressed hands
Over my contour, squeezed and stung; he first grumbles,
Working with short moves, as though he relishes the hard touch.
With infectious pain now ascending randomly
Through a twisted arm, I mention I ache – from
The skill of a deliberate and raw raid. "Where'd
You get that peculiar accent? You can just
Line it over to a two-dollar hotel.
We'll take what we need and leave you the rest."
Engines of blood pound through the avenues and tired
System of reconciliation. I can't wish, and
The rest of the drained glands of modification
Could now collapse. Are they tears uncontrollably
Growing and designing the facile outline
Of my glare? From sepia's arc, thieves, slowly mumbling

Of Madeline sleeping while I lie here dumbed, are
Mute to mute questions they'll leave so long unanswered.
Shame accompanies among the regardless
Time needed? Time to align myself, time to
Get away without being caught again,
A long time for refuge to garner a return.
Rising, I collect my keys and wallet and wipe
Tears dried to my mouth, as though I estimate
Degrees of innocence by tell-tale spots
Of assault. Yet, remarkably forward, even
Attentive to ways small features fit together
To produce primary movement, I digest
The sad remains of an incident and
Redemptively take and categorize the street.

A visitor already departs; clean, swift
Clicks to a heel distinctly cut around
An unclaimed corner and intimate the presence
Of community in a desert. My sights
Slowly redefine as though at dawn and awakened
To view seminal shapes and nascent figures in
Undegraded light. What composes a new caption
For an absurd night? Catcalls, scratches, raking that
Make risk. Reason cannot alone adjust
The indomitable status quo by simply
Demanding culprits to declare themselves bad: The
Immoral are, generally speaking, the first
To recognize their immorality. Resting
Bricks and serrated walls, neutralized by disregard,
Consciously stand and defy the dominion
Of an instructed mind that assumes only clarity
Can determine future games. Proximity blends
Again into each thought: The night's wan hue; a closed moon,
Not brimming; precepts quietly caught in
The identity of lemon peels and
Beer cans, which clog the curb – as remaining night life
Hustles to each one's darkness and a rat or two,

Clawing, hurry to a blind and two human
Eyes, glassy-blank with interest and defeat, lie
Close to the rats' craft for escape. Baptism
Does come subliminally to every episode
Of circumstantial unreality. A longish
Muscle declaring its affected condition, my
Arm throbs unevenly again; and further
Accompanying the boisterous wing, a stern
Window raps fluidly shut, coughing winter dust.
Is fear a strange wish, waiting to be consummated?

Conducting smoke, phantasms effortlessly
Puff on palliative cigarettes in a far
Corner of an alley, a jut about a building
Or beyond piles of pipe; the great cloud, like a shrewd,
Suspended spirit, thinning higher, giving part
Of night a diverse shade of gray, blends uphill
Until I can't match the impeded contrast
Between lofty darkness and whiter-drifting
Smoke – everything bound in ashen eminence.

Parking bulbs flashing. The osmotic tenderness
Of Little Car I glorify now yields to instinct
And leaves the judging to others. Estimating
A crescendo of recognition, I fumble
And deride the elusive keys; to foretaste as
Though the car were a free stroke, unfelt for too long,
I conjure up remembrance of delicious and
Infinite history to stop the deconstruction.

The car's a way to be lost – for traveling
Or exodus – a persistent cult
Of popularity. All separation has
That certain kind of possible prophecy,
And I'm satisfied to create fantasies
And then to draft a trusty path to them.
As objects will correspond to expectation,
Love, fear grow from acts of physicality;

Molding therapeutic thoughts as prospects,
The cold and the bad breath of a city
Raise my wit to wish for much better times.
I promise myself a silent road that's
Not cruel; drunks I imagine to be
Roguish; sure sounds, not inveighing my name,
With mercy in their expanse – a solitary
Train, telling a whole story with a whistle through
Singing pines. But, intrusively brusque, shrill police
Sirens jar contemplation into a compelled
And indivisible shock and persuade a blighted
Sense to notice men again, who sleep convincingly
In debris; flaring slashes through haze to hypnotize.
If poor eyes wear out, glare remains. Everything
Menaced, everything linked, ever wise
To disordered weight and distended claims.

From an accident pushed extremely to
Deceitful sarcasm, keys slip out
Of these fickle fingers, channeled into just
One healthy feat of coordination;
Still, cold panic and no sleep cut me down to think short
So that I hardly envision. Fluorescent blasts
Of light, almost burning the flesh, sizzle in their
Own electricity. Rarefied by excitement,
My hands squeeze sweat on eluding things; my eyeballs
Wetter with plot. Ultraism can't be calmed. Native
Discernment wrenched to select an exact key,
Hiding there with fingertips but inspiring error.
Over billowy, inaccurate pavement, I
Trip wildly, lying on icy asphalt breath down
And slowly muttering with inflections
For stupidity. A clot tore above the eyes;
A warm flow fills, as I wipe blood on my sleeves
That I may array patterns in perspective –
No longer subtle and human, but such
An animal, banging around inside
A paddock. Forever sleeping within

A lilliputian box-house, an attendant's numb
To business and time, while he rides unconsciousness
To limitless freedom. Once more, the key laughs,
Absconds. Then, I mock happiness. Jangling
Absolvent pieces of steel, my witless hands,
Shuddering as though they would burn away in distrust, turn
Every one. No. I bellow, "Relax or it'll
Disappear." The moment whispers that sanity
Is a matter of control. Dissipated
Nerves, uncontained – as a last chance; should the key drop, I'm
Perfectly loosed. What I must fight within to
Secure something small and lost. After gratefully
Unlocking the door and feeling the fond
Cushion's lull of placative fingers, I rebound
Tired ribs bluntly against the hard stasis
Of the steering wheel. Invading the ignition, I seek:
Low groan low in the motor deepens the drive
And grating torque; rich growling chokes
The engine. Respire, Material. Breathe
Desire into your organs. Instantly,
The tactics decline, and a diminution
Of function accelerates. Cramming at instruments,
Which command and exalt motion, I listen
To one interminable croak shrink to spurts that
Condense into a mere timorous hum.
Nothing. Silence counts the sweat-frozen lines
Of my forehead. Nothing shall gain comparison
With the self-reproaching style of frank inertia,
Machinal and determinant in default.
Remote hands decidedly limp, dormant near the dashboard.
How empty a man, if immobile. My
Eyeballs steadily burn the lids; what fading,
Conscious forms remain innate? With dots and spates
Of color darting, it seems as though buckets
Of grime, mixing hungrily with viscid blood
On my face – to boil and purify a damaged head.
Pain leaks at a disarranged cheek, where
A swollen mass now bulges inside the layer

Of assault. If I shall know any hope at all, I
Shall be devoid of unqualified pain. Thick with no
Muscle and slumped to ennui, I demur at
Current fortune or at clarion calls for help.

The day's finished. No place for return; no one to
Be sought. Acclimation, not waiting for next steps
But for compliance. With nothing else to
Attempt, then nothing else to doubt. I pry open
Cold light, as it shatters a bent, time-arrested
Focus; and stretching off weighted and hesitant limbs,
I've drooled my chin, and a string of compulsion
Menacingly dangles. Parts of stain and spit dot
The pregnable front, as I squint to set an orientation.
A rip at the pants' thigh, gas or oil, lying rude on
A pocket, dominate. When respite rearranges
Night and sifts for coalescence among fractured
Elements, involuntary forces forge
The recourse – I resist luxuriating and
Tempting languor, steady the asphalt under, and
Walk off to find a spot kindly blessed by the unknown.

What's left of unremitting distance churns
In immediate sounds I purposely commit
To continuous capture. Little Car
Then creaks through ceaseless cold like a past, rattling
In apparitional code. Adroitly, cats
Can brush across boards like mice in an alley
And tease me mean; I'm in their world, and they scratch as
I'd hit if I could if I weren't human. Other
Creatures, decayed and without decision, twisted
And abstruse – they're carrying my latent image
Street to street. What decays in those creatures with
Trembling in their veins and alcohol in
Their trembling? Like children, they don't know another
Way and can't transcend themselves – only a public
Place will become home. Moans pronounced slowly in the same
Dialect as this ache – I'm fiercely fixed

And glassy into glassy stares of others. Yes,
The guise has broken down into shadow drunks
I abhor, for I recognize the rare descent
Into Christless hunger, which, to promulgate such
A unique crucifixion, they silhouette;
To ask anybody for anything – to divide.
Rigid veins and bones near the skin I've now
Beheld regularly, it seems, all my life. Yet, somehow,
Amid the jaded paradox of haste and waste,
These old innocents can wait for someone with my
Habits, age, vanity, faded physique,
And stratagems, and they take their parts from me,
And I'm left looking for someone like my prior self.

Under the City's high mist, the safely pale
Luminance of a quiescent hotel;
The unsympathetic wood still tells a story
Of how gladly it used to summon all but, now,
Only those who dislike wisdom for a future.
Big shoes clunk off; nervous voices, stuttering,
Suddenly stop; glass, splintered randomly, splits
With ease under each footfall. A stray, crippled hound,
Who gave up home, sniffs as I arrive at the hotel
Steps, but I don't interest him, so he hobbles off
In search of approaching gratification. Light
Sprays from a tiny bulb freeze an interior,
Even illusory. Bags of men lie over
The floor; seasoned heads, then stored warm under
Burlap sacks or heavy cardboard, could agree with
A night's rush that the cold's also unconditional.
The hurriedly penciled sign sells, "A Dollar More
Upstairs"; better to accept the lowest,
But guaranteed station than to forfeit
A last reserve for more extant pleasure.
At once attracted and indifferent
To fresher craft my senses can personalize.

As soon as a plank, under some shoe, tilts uneven,
Something small squeals, leaping triumphantly over
A balustrade. Into the dark-dimpled wood wall,
An elaborate gash and, nearby, a rich, cracked
Urn can testify to the myth we all know
To be true – the god of art is no match
For the god of survival. Sour-laden clothes
And ripened-poor breaths introduce those, who,
Gathered, claim the buried floor and roar at any
Intrusive cough. I begin to step over
Bodies, systematically inert: Someone
As young as I remember I should be
And another, too apart to know the crime.

Postscript

It has been told, as a message, how loss is only
A kind of prophecy, how the meaning of vatic signs
From lower events is reducible to earth's
Incomplete form; for there's a mad style to
It all: Irony can just as well correct
The incorrigible as it can and will stifle
The powerful cries of moral creatures.

While we listen for common voices, we recall
That distance cannot alter its distance –
As our present mocks our past. Wishes defined
By place, idols of parochialism
Dissolved, and, through mist, cognition rises
So clearly it shines – with our recourse, remote and close.
A city, the hidden regions of a hamlet.

Addendum

Since readers occasionally comment on and inquire about structures to my poems, I thought I would preempt any guesswork about *January 12th, 1967*. There's nothing to hide in this respect, and a brief discussion should neither detract nor distract from the verse. At the same time, one shouldn't think there's anything sublime about the work's arrangement, unlike the mathematical purity we often associate with many pieces of music. For that latter purpose at least, poets instead have it easier. As an example, all I've really done in *January 12th, 1967* is rely on certain qualities of blank verse, adjusted with noticeable variation—not uniformly ten syllables per line at all, and there's no bevy of neat and sequential iambs as feet, either; still, the spirit of blank verse constitutes a notable part of the poem. The structure intentionally eschews adherence to repetitive, tight and formal components for a contemporary poetic work of this length; to do otherwise will, I believe, create boredom for the poet, but, more to the point, I'd rather not think how agitated today's reader would become at the monotony.

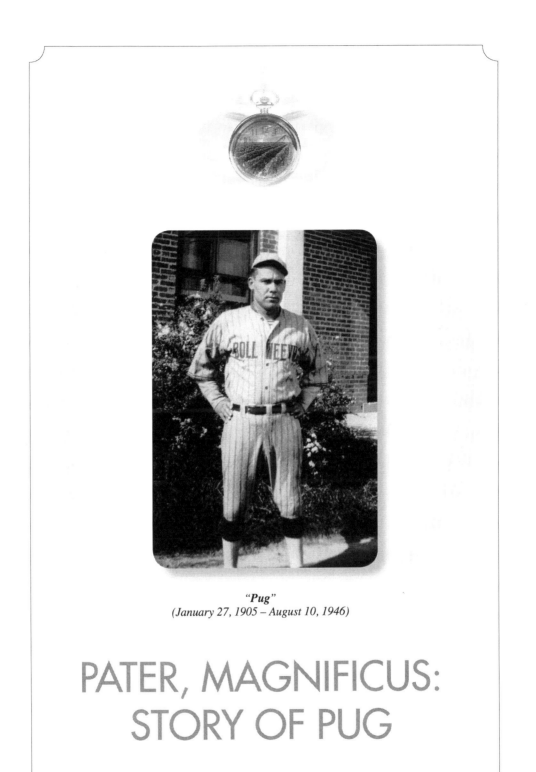

"Pug"
(January 27, 1905 – August 10, 1946)

PATER, MAGNIFICUS: STORY OF PUG

Pater, Magnificus: Story of Pug

Preface

The search for another, long deceased and long obscured, can be corrective but resistive, revelatory but blind. That's the occasion for Pater, Magnificus: Story of Pug. *From the beginning, the path overgrew, in alternating phases, with myth and muteness, but it was never stale or uninviting. So, how does a son, who had been much too young, find a father, who had disappeared much too soon and who leaves a track mostly in memories with those left behind? Warily, grittily through storytellers of every kind and by a world, wherever extant, of letters, histories, memorabilia, scrapbooks and notable snippets. Initially composed in a somewhat different version more than two decades ago, this verse then bore another title but contained the same quest. The poem relies on elastic rhyme, a form discussed in the Author Comments.*

"Pug" or, as known to some, "Slick," my father, John Chester Johnson, was born January 27, 1905 in Pike City, Arkansas, a spot with such a small population that, even now, it barely exists. Pug's birth came less than eight months after his parents wed in a nearby hamlet, Murfreesboro, some nine miles southwest of Pike City. The marriage took place with no family members present as witnesses, the bride and groom sitting aboard a horse drawn wagon in the midst of strangers from a Presbyterian congregation, taking a break from a worship service. Pug would be the oldest of three children—one brother, one sister.

Before I reached the age of two, Pug had died from intestinal cancer at 41; thus, all my memories of him were forged through the eyes of others, including my mother, who never remarried or dated after his death. Notwithstanding the secondhand nature of the contacts, a careful blend of factual history and many stories can unearth a person, if one is willing to spend the time mining.

One disappointment, for sure, can't be overcome—I have no stories to tell of Pug's childhood. It seems he must have sprung directly from birth to college and thereafter—without a few, decent vignettes or parables to explain a little of his early journey. We learn when we're quite young that stories convey an essence mere facts and declarations can only envy. It's a genuine loss that I have no portrayals or details of Pug's opening life—answers to otherwise easy questions. Did Pug ever get sent home from grade school for disrupting class or for fighting (as I did, more than once)? What did a teenager conceivably do on weekends in georgic Arkansas? Pug's first girlfriend, high school loves? What were they like? I'm afraid the story of Pug shall be told starting mostly midstream.

Pug grew up in southeast Arkansas at Wilmar, located a hundred miles east of his birthplace, thirty miles west of the Mississippi River and some twenty-five miles or so north of Louisiana. The place, like Pike City, embodied more of a small village than a small town, though Wilmar at the time retained its own public education system, which extended through high school. Pug's father, John, the railroad depot agent and a local farmer, anticipated and received ample respect, if not downright obeisance from Pug and the other siblings, and the mother, Ora, wasn't one for whom a child could seek and readily find refuge or a hug. Pug proved to be more than a decent student, finishing the ninth through the twelfth grades in three years—all the time, displaying athletic gifts.

Although he attended three colleges, Pug never graduated. Of course, he wasn't without intelligence but possessed, in those years, a mercurial change of purpose—after college, Pug moved from place to place and job to job. Over a handful of years, he played minor league baseball; clerked for the Missouri Pacific Railroad, both in Vidalia, Lousiana and McGehee, Arkansas, where he courted Opal, his future wife, and which was, not coincidentally, only a short distance from Wilmar; ran (lost) for a County office seat in 1932; worked as a foreman for highway construction; drove a bus and rose to bus dispatcher before turning to the sale of life insurance.

Unfortunately, I'm afraid Pug carried a full measure of the conventional religious and racial bias prevailing through that region of the country at the time. For example, a nickname that stuck to him at the University of Arkansas and Hendrix College was the damaging and pervasive "N" word white Southerners have pejoratively made famous in reference to African-Americans. The various, realistic reasons Pug would have been dubbed "N" are all overtly racist, so I'll just leave the nickname as a historical fact and go on from here. At some point, by informal bequest, probably in response to my immutable interest, I was granted my father's "memories" book, which includes photographs, press clippings, and ad hoc mementos and covers a period ending about his mid-twenties; however, there's no mention, at all, of his early life before graduation from high school. Given an especially prominent spot in Pug's memories book is a poem, written either by him or a friend, that is rabidly anti-Al Smith, the 1928 presidential candidate of the Democratic Party, who became, during the election campaign, controversial simply for being Catholic. The poem also takes general swipes at both Catholics and Jews. I occasionally muse over Pug's possible response if he had understood his daughter-in-law, my wife, would be Jewish.

The most disguisable of traits—one's true "religious" sentiments—are hard, if not impossible, to confirm, certainly from a long distance, a handicap I face. By all accounts, Pug must have gathered his father's religious convictions for his own. John reversed from kinetic atheism as a young man, when he and a roving band of allied rebels sometimes broke up revival meetings in Texas and Arkansas by riding horses through churches and camps, to a profound conversion, to hear it told, in the tradition of St. Paul's encounter on the road to Damascus. Apparently, as far as I can tell, Pug didn't resist his father on the subject of religion and never looked back.

The men (not all, but certainly enough) in my father's family frequently favored alcohol, and Pug wouldn't be a stranger to it either, drinking fulsomely at times for a vivifying spirit and other ventures of manhood. After "party" nights with the boys, Pug often paid a heavy penalty when his wife, Opal, forced Pug to sleep with his head leaning toward the open window—even in winter. Opal is known to have taken a swing at Pug once he returned home should he exhibit especially bad behavior or judgment. Though small, she could land a heavy blow, for Pug, at the end of such a night, didn't have residual wits about him to duck. As a son of the father, I drank my fair share before I gave up the juice entirely—I should have done it sooner.

A secret. One had to be there to understand. Undoubtedly, a big secret. The children couldn't live with it. The shoot who came closest to breaking free of its constraints was Pug. The sister, crushed by it into a caretaker role, never left the confines of the Johnson house. The brother, who endured prolonged bouts with alcohol over his lifetime, submitted to the secret's dictates in his twenties after brief forays toward freedom's mountain. I do not know the nature, but I do know the leviathan size of the secret. It was so large that it spread into the next generation, but I had the good luck, fear and anger to stay as far away from it as I conceivably could. By the time I came along, however, its force had dissipated so much that it could be outrun, overrun and outsmarted without even a meager, psychological blow, if one recognized the value of escape—and a couple of grandchildren did.

Pug had just hit the longest home run ever at the Wilmar baseball field— now 27, he was a little older than the rest of the players on the field that day. Someone said the ball traveled close to five hundred feet. "This pack of townies will always exaggerate," Pug thought to himself. Still, for some odd reason, he wouldn't keep his mind on the game. Questions he'd never resolved kept inserting themselves into Pug's concentration, even when he should pay more attention, as catcher, to the directions he gave pitchers. Why did Dad have so little contact with his own brothers? Goodness, Pug's uncles were well-known—Cecil had just been elected chief justice of the Arkansas Supreme Court and Dick, county judge and state representative from Little River County. Why did Dad move so far away from his own family? Not the sort of thing his father talked about. Pug just had to continue to live with questions.

Pug and Opal married before he dove into life insurance. They had dated off and on for about five years—"off" while Pug was away several months a year with minor league baseball. She just didn't recognize herself as a stay-at-home-and-wait kind of gal. Finally, one night, Pug told her if she didn't agree on a wedding date, he'd just walk off the porch and she'd never see him again. Opal's parents thought more of Pug than they did for most of their own seven children. Pug and Opal got married on September 27, 1931.

The selling of life insurance appealed to Pug, and apparently he was pretty good at it. But soon, another idea percolated. Once Pug started to reveal talent as a considerable salesman of life insurance in and around McGehee, he found communication with the company's home office in Tennessee less helpful and timely than he believed prudent and possible. So, Pug sought a meeting with the company president and convinced him that Pug should take on a position that previously hadn't existed, home office representative to areas where the company's life insurance policies were sold. Over the next several years, Pug and Opal conducted odysseys from Nashville, Tennessee across parts of the eastern United States; they were later joined by my older brother, John Maxie, born in 1938.

Of course, Pug had been an athlete—football, but mostly baseball in college and, for a few years, as I've said, in the minor leagues. A family story relayed he didn't rise to the "Big Show" (with farm teams then more controlled on a geographic allotment system) because a headline player, another Arkansas catcher, occupied the spot with the host team. More than likely, the rumor is a fabricated myth, but it's fun for conversation, nonetheless. Normally, good athletes are imprinted by their sport. In Pug's case, he liked to try to hit home runs (all his life), he liked to put on the catcher's gear (always a snappy dresser, a feature I didn't inherit), and he would run out ground balls down the first base line (one should do that sort of thing to be successful at selling life insurance).

Pug preferred to perform in front of an audience. I guess athletics permitted the trait—to be enviably before a crowd. He participated in plays during college, and family pictures show he sought to be the focus (maybe, even a bit of a dandy). He'd tell a multiplicity of jokes and act out, gravitating to and inspiring pranks. Later, as an insurance home office representative, his job consisted mainly of motivating the troops (the company's sales forces along the eastern seaboard), and he must have been effectual at writing and giving speeches. From the time I could read, Opal passed out copies of Pug's compositions. Then, as I grew a little older, it remained always crucial to her that I thought those pieces exceptional.

A few months after Pug and the family moved from Nashville to Chattanooga, a location that gave him a much better launching pad for the job, I was born in September, 1944. I'm convinced I'd been an accident—nearly seven years after the birth of the first child, who apparently had been treated like an only child. Then, some six months later in March, 1945, Pug accepted a better position with another insurance company, this one with home offices in Galveston, Texas.

In certain respects, Pug fostered contradictions. At the height of his insurance career in Tennessee and Texas, the income allowed for maids, nice clothes, attractive two story homes, new cars, and plenty of vacations and travel. Although he secured this abundance through life insurance, it was discovered, at his death, that Pug carried precious little on himself, so that his wife and two boys survived mostly on social security, supplemented by occasional cuttings of timber from a small tree farm he had left to Opal.

When home in Wilmar, Pug orchestrated a routine. One component, shoe cleaning. Applying toothpicks, he prodded out dirt in the crevices and perforations of his shoes. He also made it a point to wear overalls and a hat (he loved hats, a love I share)—he knew the part. Then, Pug would stroll the unpaved roads, paths and trails throughout the hamlet to renew friendships and catch up on the latest local news. He treated the time as though he were watching the grass grow.

Pug did not have a chance to get entirely settled into the new job before calamity hit. By early 1946, Pug, constantly losing weight, confronted a serious medical problem. Yes, his weight, as a matter of course, rose and fell routinely—the extreme variation being an upshot of eating binges, which were logically replaced, in turn, by severe reduction efforts. No, this was something else.

In March, 1946, following a business trip that had been scheduled for eleven weeks but was completed in seven, Pug returned to Wilmar. Family members voiced concern over his appearance, ashen and drawn; all being accustomed to his felicity, spontaneity and vitality, Pug's behavior shifted to the subdued and somewhat detached. After a series of tests were conducted in both Little Rock and Galveston, a preliminary diagnosis determined that a growth in the colon had rapidly enlarged. Pug consequently underwent in May, 1946 an operation in Galveston, during which the surgeons discovered a wide-spread, fully developed and incurable cancer. They closed Pug back up and told the news to immediate family members, who had gathered at the hospital, except for Pug's father, who, instead, for his own special, if not peculiar reasons, stayed home, several hundred miles away in Arkansas. Once hearing the report, Pug decided, on the spot, he wanted to be in Wilmar for the time remaining.

At his parents' home, Pug went down quickly. There was not a lot of talking, chiefly, I believe, as a result of the morphine, which he consumed willingly and copiously to reduce but not kill the pain. At first, Pug ate and conversed with the family, but then he gradually and inevitably faded into himself and his pain and his morphine. Not surprisingly, battles ensued over Pug between Opal and her in-laws, battles creating scars that abided long after he died, although the conflicts, at the time, were quietly kept under visible control—away from Pug.

The doctors in Galveston predicted right after the May operation that he could possibly live with the cancer for three months. Actually, he passed away only five days short of the three months. Pug became fully unconscious Tuesday, August 6th, and died August 10th, 1946. Pug's body returned to his parents' home on the 11th for one more day—in an open casket so that mourners could come to his parents' home and show their respects. The funeral service and interment occurred Monday, August 12th.

Around this time, I believe my first recallable consciousness surfaced—brief, but clear recollections of an African-American woman watching over me in my grandparents' backyard, as many people arrived and departed—the recollections too crisp and precise, too perfect, if you will, for mere imaginations, derived from repetitive hearing of similar accounts. I remember the corner of the yard and the clothing and rich face of the woman charged with my care; also, the fence, even the colors.

Pug's tombstone, for an inexplicable reason, had been entrusted, in every respect, to his sister, Kathleen, who customarily exhibited remarkable flares for the unusual, expressive, and oftentimes immoderate. First, a rather huge and classic broken column found its way onto the tombstone—ancient Egyptians employed analogous columns to indicate the deceased had been cut down in the prime of life; after Alexander the Great conquered Egypt and Ptolemic rule reigned there, the same motif also began to spring up on many Greek monuments. Of course, this particular column for Pug created a lot of pointing and stares at the vicinal Oakland Cemetery. Next, Kathleen proceeded with a poem, "The Death of the Flowers," by William Cullen Bryant, as she exchanged all the feminine pronouns for masculine ones in a concluding quatrain, which then became the commemorative words, adjacent to the broken column. In all, artfully done, if a bit askew to conventional fare. For no other reason than this, I think it proved to be a good thing—Pug would hardly be forgotten in local lore with those pregnant and quite visible remembrances, appearing in the very front burial plot, whenever a hearse or mourners or friends or family of any departed entered the cemetery.

For much of the first couple of decades, I adhered to the idealized version of Pug, borne by surviving family members. Since Opal, my brother and I settled a few years later, following Pug's death, within several miles of Wilmar, the fictionalized recounting was continually reinforced at an early age, but I finally resolved over time that this version constituted the most demeaning one, which left out many marks revealing the authentic person, the true person—pieces didn't fit. OK, maybe he memorized large sections of the New Testament; maybe he strove to be an adoring husband, caring father, and dutiful son; and maybe he became a 32nd or 33rd degree mason (whatever that is), but he was something else, too. The marks I learned later that helped to refine him—the flamboyance, the excesses, the rough humor, the drinking, the enlivened communion among men, the religious and racial prejudice—escaped the ideal; without them, he wasn't real. I sought Pug as he had been. The search evolved into my own curious odyssey, astounding and somewhat fitful. I'll never find him really, of course, but that's hardly the point—at least now, I can compare notes with him and know Pug is trying to give me a straight answer.

∽◌∾

Yes, I'm ready to make peace, Dad,
       Are you? If so, please take the several steps down from
       Lofty tiers. It's not a little embarrassing, for there's no
Doubt my friends frown on heights of this
       Sort. Come now, Dad, we've both been caught short, so,
       Come down, and let's talk for a spell; oh, we'll first get
The perfunctory set of manners out of the way, and I'll
Say we count on each other's point of view about any

Old subject to help us be what we declare,
       As the case may be. Then, we'll wear casually the longer
       Sense of tragedy to assure the other that something exciting
Is, at our expense, about to happen; and again,
       We'll stare to measure the distance falling uncomfortably
       Between us. For sure, we deal much better with facts:
Dates of birth and death, who lived with whom,
Acts of violence, storms and flood, scores, aunts

And uncles, and the like, as we can't decide
       On any absolute to lead. Frankly, I won't apologize for not
       Forging well ahead, and let's not discuss why this is all too
Old, our trying again to reconcile divides
       That break apart these generations. Dad, I've come to assume
       We're dependent on each other's struggle and part; indeed,
My own wins were to correct your defeats, and
The reverse may also prove as direct and true. That

Is what this close plot is all about, isn't
       It, a chance to amend the ways we feel toward the other so to
       Quicken the speed and get on with our own business? And more,
Since only the living can set the sins of
       The dead right, the better I speak and think of you and your
       Saving lore, the more you have left standing for any purpose –
More demand for colonies and conditions you
Have on this world that must favor your warts

And the rest, too, controlling those who have
       Reason to know your side and who dispose of and endow you
       Faithfully to the last days, remnant of survivors. . .For we mostly

Expect the future to be a bit more generous
    In its respect for memory than it normally is; that's the twit,
    Coming to terms with nonchalance, while not succumbing
To a natural incline of regard for style or
Other gestures. I'd like to ascribe my stubborn

Miles solely to you, but from what I've read,
    To describe it that way wouldn't do it justice; though it comes
    Homemade, you can't lay it even to fathers as a group, either.
But, maybe, you've helped refine it into size
    Without being abstract; otherwise, how could it mean so much
    So often? If it weren't for the swell to get an answer to such
Riddles, I would probably swallow and leave
Well enough alone, and you could stay dead,

And I would continue along with a knack
    For matching my choice and charters to the fixed, leading
    To standard track and prompting me to invoke well-traveled
And slightly boring rites. Let's admit it:
    We're unwilling to talk about our own miscues – why, it gets
    Reliable and comic the way we like to put nearby sins on the
Other's doorstep and strike an elegant
Scheme by attributing our lower traits

To someone else's nature and bad judgment.
    I lately accept the odd rumor that children take after their
    Parents, but I'm not adept at knowing exactly how it flows,
Or how true it is also remains uncertain
    And unclear, but as a fair rule, parents believe it more completely
    Than the children, which principle has more to do with conflicts
Between self and a will to be remembered
Than with any dispute over the degree of

Reign and myths of one generation visited
    On a succeeding one. There are inspired twists and skills I've
    Acquired you could find jagged or intolerable, maybe affected.
The person who wakes up in sin one morning
    To view himself operating in a pocket of power may have little
    Mind or courage for it or a willingness to bear another

Faded and blank edifice or a danger
The cloud of mere image will yet raise.

The keys to change never altered our chance
    To function as father and son; coarse memories hardly lurched as
    We heard soft tolerance, a modus operandi continuously waiting
In unity to provide delicious notes and effects.
    Now, that's all turned – we've both reached a critical point for words:
    We know better than to rely on facile doctrines, which return to
Haunt and show those who have used them the lesser
Upshots that come from simplified ease. But almost

Seduced, let me explain – I miss the hard
    Wars we've had, and they remain as a reference, like glad tunes
    No one forgets and everyone hums to sad completion once the
First note is struck. None ever said anger
    Wasn't one of the least remote and safer moods
    To play; it is certainly an apparent trove; for without
A splash of anger, I wonder if I could feel a
Pledge of passion toward you at all. Still, I

Know they say anger fills the other side
    Of submission, and that's the wild and subconscious ride I receive
    Over this new plain; how anger shows its face contemptuously
As the maimed mask of control, once bared,
    Falling victim to guilt and default over again. . .you understand
    Famously, for you've seen me falter mad under direct and those
Wily questions only fathers could possibly
Ask; you foresee a decline ever at the very

Time I think I am being unique, but canny
    And unflawed; you saw behind my sublime notion and defense foreign
    Troops encircling the endangered house, but I could not see them from
The worlds I had not yet tried. All remained
    Silent until my disguise and ruse were disclosed, and I succumbed
    To distant ties, but you could see it all coming, immutable and
Unopposed, couldn't you, Dad? And yet, you were
Quiet, resting on the rubric that anything you had

Said would bias your son against the full
 State I should finally have to judge. So, instead, you chose to
 Be flush-voiced earnestly about your own early triumphs, as one
Generation cannot relay to the next how to fail
 Without the use of visual ads. . .On pretext, one of us should
 Tell a joke right now – it would break the tight and ambiguous
Wheel; but this age has never been blessed with
Much of a sense of humor, which may trace to

Our limits and borders. I understand you
 Practiced humor to recruit compliance when you couldn't
 Prove your point any other way. . .Our generation disproving
The truth that an argument or a license can be
 Won calmly by a marvelous sleuth of amusement only – of course,
 Not overdone as an intentional ploy; this age enjoys being rough
And combative, as though anger alone proves selfhood,
Or, equally, we wait to behave with resolution to outlive

All other accounts more loudly than if we can
 Rebound or not, or if we, as gamblers, are right or not. It must
 Be our need for rarity that got us into this shape, for victory matters
Less if one can save face or escape with a single
 Move – indeed, if the image should cohere intact, loss will
 Appear more wanted than victory, unnoticed, unexposed.
The gains of comedy shall still work atop, for
We haven't lost the thrill to swill a few bits of

Irony to a delight. I think we do, however,
 Miss subtlety more than we confess, performing literal and highly
 Stark measures and orders, while often, I notice, we warm to old
Masters of indirection for laughs or art or
 Music without a controlled wish to imitate them; by what excuse
 Will we enjoy most of the things we refuse to practice or elevate
For private models? It must have something
To do with our linear bent: Anything that just can

Not be proven has to be riddled, but anything
 That can be fully understood as proof no longer fascinates nor entertains
 Us. Sir, we are silly, of course, I know that, but what would you have

Done if you had to compete with infinite noise,
    Addictive films, digital speed, granded cars, women wrestlers, and
    Millionaire and branded athletes to get even a nod of attention?
You would have ended up looking pretty
Ridiculous, too. Yes, in unison, rational types

Suffer at the playful quirk in every age and
    Find they've served the very gods they had wished to overwhelm.
    Let's not fall for what we remember; rather, let's dwell on the
Reward of what is possible, for a recall creates
    The dream that somehow history can be changed, and we're not
    Up to that retreat; leave the extreme to the promptly fainthearted,
Who clutch at any belief so as not to be so variable
By being too fixed. What is past is past, and

Dwelling on it resets the little faith we have
    In ourselves. At the risk of slow wit, I waited, for your
    Sake, on schemes I'd like to pursue, and I took in this
Order: First, the strike of gentle moments to
    Count; next, laws to nudge toward an amateur and lighter
    Dig; and then, one viewpoint drawing calm when misfortune
Blows for fun like a devilish and tormenting tragedy
Over ordinary ways. I admit I cannot argue that

Deep ache won't come along with wonder –
    Indeed, many were the ways you molded my headlong and mettlesome
    Accents when I had no idea the shaping was, of course, in place. Yet,
Even you, Dad, may be much of an illusion,
    For I have taken on so many of those desires to call on something
    lost and not to find. Still, there's likely more that bids us together
Than we've told each other is here. I realize
It's hard to believe simply for the two of us,

As we're treading to remain separately our
    Own persons, while we don't cede a particular inch for fear of
    Appearing weak and unabled before them who flinch with
Suspicion in the face of our stumbles and
    Stammers. But there are others who recognize grace in our sins,
    And we laughingly grant at these times that foibles may commit

Themselves at will when we're not on notice
Or when we wish to settle a score and catch

Our competing angels off guard. If smarter, we'd
    Draw on borrowed fruits fallen between us, but since we resist victory
    In favor of familiarity, we reach to save our more preserved selves,
Not for those who linger to silence, who, not
    Like one of us, take a visitor or two, without obligation or
    Correction, and who do not need to assert for themselves that
They too perform as we perform or fail or as we
Lose sight of long distant form and forges. . .

Oh, logic must desert the reason when the world
    Around us means rhetoric. . .So, tell me, Father, how does one
    Handle anger for family affairs? I'm not just talking about earthy
Wellings I sometimes have for you that bristle
    Behind the ear. No doubt, it's also the close effect with an intimate
    Kind and thorns. . .and how a kaleidoscopic phrase, an architecture,
Shall twist and spin in rack fortune; at such
Times, demonic claims shall rise and list a

Possessive head and select outrageous portions
    And bodies to feed as though they spread like consumptive voids which
    We alone can satisfy. Do you sense what I mean? The absence of
Abundant control in this family may be a spur to
    Berate torques of anger, but slowly. How can I stay so long attending
    This trait of madness for less ready ends? No, anger still flicks favorably
Upon magic to prevail, whether it's delivered
On time or not. But there's no obscure walking

Around a heated pulse or sidling up to its presence;
    Rather, you break down walls and fall through doors to reach
    The creature face to face, to govern cataracts and process lore.
For us, it's the trick to let forms of delusion
    Unfolding their rage run their course, as we discover here
    And there a glinting cue that conveys a new clarity, and
That's beauty, I suppose. We can
Oddly invoke star-crossed havoc for

Each of the innocent bystanders, who do not know
    The script or the cause a breach has occurred, who are singled
    Out adjacently for attack. But as we both agree, this and that
For personal acts are hardly ever balanced, and
    Each curt observer, from an average peek, owns this fact too well,
    Preferring a march to seek innocence and the onslaughts of open
Fields, easy seasons. What do you suggest? A
Good deal of excess grind and unrest cannot

Alone decide the prices we're willing to pay.
    I've gained in a swarm over us in a doubled sense, for I have
    Children, who hold me in more safeless awe than they should,
Though if they don't, they must withdraw
    Harmed behind a shadow and fail to learn the values of myth.
    We both saw the untombed soon summoned to inspire and
Fulfill even the meanest talent; otherwise, most
Simply go about their time still electing the

Smallest examples of human fairs and daybreak,
    Second half of first signs, foresight prepared and written for
    Sunsets. I'm not opposed, anymore than you, to children believing
In the yet, undeveloped works of a father –
    Yes, of even a child's matchless blessing and stopovers. Indeed,
    They can't displease, as I'm treated with naïve and effulgent nature –
It's the common end of myth that those little whims
That entirely satisfy through conventional law will

Be attached to a lesser world we create for our
    Narrow and very odd tales. Uncurled alone, I grew more like you
    Over the years; even though we disown it and follow variant plots,
When all is said and shown, age does
    Create more shared nicks and knocks than we care to conjugate.
    There are discussions we could never have had elsewhere, some
Years ago, now available to us, as an
Unexceptional life burned out the frontiers

Or flames of political views that separated
    Us then. I can now talk and prefer another line and stand for it without

Searching for part truths on which we awkwardly compromise as a
Routine order to size up the bigger job of
    Finding, with small regret, we dislike seeing ourselves in each other
    And would rouse fresh stories to maximize the manicured and mocking
Contrasts. Oh, we seek arrays on the spot to
Blind us from true motives and hidden displays.

And lately, I feel a vein to tout gross designs
    That heavily endow the features of my normalcy. It helps to
    Have children, as they wish so completely that their legends
Shall depart from those of slighter rubs; for
    Children, as a rule, have a heart to wish for things huge
    And small to be captured in monoliths and by behemoths.
It helps to have children, who give us
Cover for being more commonplace than

We thought we'd ever be; they laden me with
    Reasons I should defend the old radii between old friends, who once
    Heard my thick speech about natural law, world freedom and the
Inherent vista of each self. How much
    I believed myself to any extent even then I don't recognize. Here, I
    Sit, waiting waywardly with impatient sides for you and a matrix of
Blessings to happen, to leave a numbered life
(And to measure it as closure) for a full-swing

And blood-tempered range of wilder tendencies that
    Find their name in opinion and choice. Only photographs to frame
    You by, as in base, sad ways, I would objectively fold your outline,
Like any other subject caught in precise lines,
    Begrudged for their precious portions, reflected in facsimile.
    Yet, the replicas never learned the uncorrected remains, while
I hallowed upon familiar, but remote
Origin, leaving my domain there amazed

That I was somehow destined to become:
    Disappearing acts are hard I would vow, if not impossible, to follow.
    Just ask anyone in a greater act, and they'll tell you so, and we're no
Exception. I longed to emulate the image

You were, after such a quick exit put a stamp, an imprint of special
    Clause, fit upon your bones; only later did the moist folly and
Darkened eye of rare success for the
Attempt arrive. So, I quit trying and soon

Left to tell of the pleasures of fleeing a common
    Season played between unevens. And yet, so, I, in many respects,
    Managed; I think, by now, I have become, first of all, a few moments
Of my own. From this bridge alone, I'm
    Able to talk to you with mere minor discomfort, no severe slant;
    Only equals converse, unequals chatter. Thus, we can report
It's a good deal healthier now, since the
Lions have crawled back into their caves

With no late meal, the snakes have disappeared,
    The ravens are silenced, and the hinges and rages of your coffin no
    Longer screech and whine for relief from the expanse of pressure you
Exert to pursue an unfaithful and undutiful son.
    Besides, you're more tolerable in a seemingly close hereafter, as I give
    You less distance to uphold me; indeed, the rival sides of my answer
Would have you do nothing right now,
While I lounge in a newfound neighborhood

Of slow liberty. Let there be no mistake:
    Freedom's near yet another rule, where we often cannot tell the two
    Apart; conscious of freedom, we languor and soon choose to take
Those turns that tempt us to be entrapped
    And to break away from all acute liberty; a problem of balance and
    Weight has always been the matter. It's too private, these taller stands
At replaying old events – I wish I could have said
This or that without stressing deadened wood;

Or I had not risen to the gift of your challenge.
    Private resurrections, no fad; private haste, private lies: They, perhaps
    Fabled emphatics, for we simply add nothing if they do not survey
And improve the quality of our map for
    Others, as trite as that rather proves to sound. Everything I do limiting
    My conversation gathers to my exile and fallow walls, to my private

And exclusive world, where those more
Reclusive feats congregate with loss, jagged

Rocks and denuded brush, where little rain
    Is felt and little sunshine passes. Time evaporates and does stain, and I
    Have meant to work exposure for select places, but I went about it
The wrong way, never charting around to
    Facial, fontal or fructive tracts to match them to a better airing: There are
    Always mistakes to be countered or confirming goals to be attained and
Freedoms to be extended and sins to be
Denied victory. The secret and detained

Garden remains unsolved, even as an aside, as we
    Become public when pleasures multiply, circulating through an ever-
    Widening view. We tell stories of fate for the sake of arrival. But to
Privacy, all we've really done is reduce the number
    Of available prospects. So often, then, an extreme notion yields an early
    Surrender – tell me again, Dad, why fathers try to get so far away? It's
Not your special escape nor single legend – I do
The same and leave them fluttering among the

Lightness of a callow life. It may be established
    To treat them undoubtedly, their selfhood left to strengthen and entreat
    Our greater likeness, though we go so long in filling a detached kind
Or flatten out our ways 'til they're little more than
    A mere service we bear or a dry effort in the role where
    Everyone assigns us – a name we share and wear. To enrich
Our seams, nearer than to admit, any
Old touch can guard against the grate

Of what is essentially grave tempest and hollow noise.
    One would think, of course, we'll need not follow straight lines within
    Family ties, for things peculiar happen the closer families become. . .
We chase surprising rolls of change only if they're
    Controlled by a boundless and stranger text. Here, by being probable, we're
    Never free to those whom we know best. Who's perplexed? It seems
We seek to urge a maddening, if nurtured, craze
And fault raised by a wicked and awkward phrase

That has been presumed for us – without our
     Consent? And even more at hand, Dad, is the curious report of
     Those children who measure and wane and who do not inquire
Around secret webs where we sit sanely and
     Let logic running high encircle our styles of wit. I understand
     Why I lure the removed ones to a chorus of our duet, our ghostlike
Sighs in the presence of repeated tunes.
So, in my indulgence, I try to maneuver

Dialogue and quiet favor to result in license
     And exult for the reckless places I have been sent, I have shared,
     And I have taken. Ageless terrain you and I, dilated, trace and
Cross again without resistance; time
     Whispers in quickened pace, and about this hour, we are caught,
     Formless, by the gathered acceleration of regret. Even as I talk,
My bare hands grow dry, and the thickness of my
Blood declines, and the cold wears featureless and

Vain. There's no comfort then that age will
     Be unaggressive and unvictorious – we can't but wield time as much
     For a token as for a retreat; it shall also ensue and fit us with
Site and lessons, as we boast of fakes and
     Falls and the many creatures we were long ago. . .And those so
     Young taking us at last at our word. Who can know the times
Any better? Tell me, who should I
Count to be ready for the abundant way

Things really are? I'd like to rely on you,
     For blood is not far apart and thicker than water, so they
     Say, though I'm not so sure. Common threads stand firm,
Which neither of us can deny, though no
     Good spot can give a good cause to watch over my own
     Past. Can we persuade my own progeny lines to cast ahead
And then forego my hidden and receding
Claims? At what point do I throw all this

Out and stop following and start fronting?
     When I have caught up with heralding answers as to why the shroud

Of history does not pledge ever to release the future for fear of
Disclosing something other than loud
Anonymity? Relax, I tell us, from simplemindedness of it all; but
Deciding not to take a lead, do I lose the chance to succeed at loss?
In any case, nothing now seems spare or content,
For some were meant in this world to scurry

After ease in a softer beat, and, of course,
They're successful. Please, just ask, and I'll tell you how
Very unstressed I am, I write, as I'll be, all the while – set,
Like a tighter muscle, in straits, and, yet, so,
I'm very subdued? Yes, I'll confirm it, I'm a fraud – here,
There, plotting margins impressive and protecting signs,
Wishing to think back so you'll tell the
Reason one thing happens and some

Others won't. But does it matter should
It be you or I, since this conversation, we don't doubt, will not
Depend on which one of us is speaking but on how we intend
To allow the other to sing of a venture
He wants to explore and avow, while it's taking him someplace
Where the two of us, in the midst, can meet at a favorite tract?
Old prerogatives pass by, a message barely
Clears, and chances are food will continue

To have a gamey taste while I argue for
The next meal I believe we should take. We must talk even
With shallow swaths, even as we wish to skip away and be
Heard above the sheer din of self-regard.
One can then be spurred to mutter that doubt and retrenchment
May mean the first moves of conspicuous truth. Why, Father,
We pout and worry over those matters
About which we do little and know less. . .

But I gullibly keep on learning. . .also
Pontificate to silence and offer silently complaints that some haven't
Altered to my lesson or rubric, my espousing full-well errant whimsy
That if they did, I must then find more

Equally wrong with them, restructured amid the image I'd mark that
    Needs a fix. Anyway, who are we to play an All-Father, who has
Already faced rumblings that I can't keep my
Own provocations, alongside snarling dogs,

And my own weaker tries under wraps? And
    If nonchalant, we can't assure by being impassive, but then being
    Nonchalant by being righteous and vulturish to those we seek to convince.
Oh, it's a curious fact the older, more dimpled I
    Have become, the less I worry about a precious purity, disguising
    Pieces of itself in drab, rapid form. It's not the success that matures us,
It's glad failure with fury and melodrama; so,
When I total the sum of my faults, the formula

For peace does not mind the failure of
    Many so much. I still lear and worry over loose strangers who will
    Burn and who, to defer toward safer times, do not agree with my
Patterns for the way things were and are.
    Now, I have a tale-filled son of my own – I think he hides the
    Doubtless echoes of a father as one act of refuge much better
Than I did. There's surely no defense for an
Exchange in parts, as, in turn, a nearby view

Will contend that there were far fewer myths
    With which he had to tend; and for his own good, it's been easier, I
    Suppose, for the dead stayed dead when they passed through, and
Outcomes were a checked and lasting close. I
    Now worry his world may be so normal by self-control he'll miss
    The fairs of obsession, though they're awash with danger, abyss,
Hellhound, and doom. It's a sounder bet, we
Found, to be slightly insane; if not, life's tamed

To no extremes and to boring walks; an angle
    Askew gives off a better chance to lay bare clinging shadows that lurk
    In the dark expanse of our abiding, often predatory secrets and schemes.
He imitates my stride until the hour his friends
    Pose, among the rest run, a local threat, for they alone compete with
    Burnished, home-down skill; presence, old or young, is harder regimens

To spoil by counterfeit; even he, fresh and now brave
Before the plain, also says grass and hearty words

Cannot be reduced to any sly cliché, to a
    Light epigram that carries no proud weight or occasion. But you're
    Confirmed and complete, Dad, no halfway artist, no siree, and all
The more singular, holy and honored because
    You've raced the long road; yet, I've heard the histories and murmurs you
    Were no saint, just jestful and fun-loving, in levities, like an animated
Sizzle, who'd make others laugh and forget
Themselves a sad corner; celebrated and

Labeled gift, you drank too much for
    Laughs and lift, as someone stuck your open face through an
    Open window while you slept to stop the ballad. Now, the
Trace of the told tales became drama,
    The enduring place of unearthed clues, and I hum to the tune
    That we never exert so much loss as we do at some moment of a
Story's end; but we know the verse best if
True, having glared for years at clear-cut

Lies, which gather while we roughly finger the
    Truth and take aim from facets and whirls. Father, we choose enough
    Rhetoric and selfish phrase to profess we each cannot be led again by
Likely cabals, once more bending and receding
    Back to Original Sin; we're all most often best left to find the track
    For our own answers and to seek out our own deft lessons, for the
wrongs and rules of the past can be played
Only upon a given set of notes in the margin.

I wish I could have amassed a good deal of
    Rumor to the contrary, but the more personal races we try have better use:
    What we discover and where it rises, what works in our hands, what takes
Root – we alone decide. The old male story
    Within this wholly veteran family will not halt here with me, Dad, though
    I often wish it could for the sake of the rest. Anyone can fault my son for
Merely passing along a line by falling for my
Song as I have done, with only modest class,

Reciting your refrain. His passage, I pray, shall
    Be diverse and native, mostly humane and tender, subtle, even exact,
    But humorous and prophetic, even to a loss; and so, I'll simply not
Now propound nor incite his story at will or at all
    Until he molds the swell of his own voice around those famous songs
    And chants – a lilt with convincing choice, performing creed and
The longer sounds of freedom. At these times, try
As I might, I know I'll never be more than a son.

HOME

Home

1

The lonely hours   when all is gone
to work out language for the content,
to incite reproach for something simply, wrongly done:
    A voice too loud
    a light phrase for comedy veering
    rude horn
    indecent breath
    and low accomplishments   are cited. . .
        I didn't make my own –
        I made someone else's mistake;
but still contending,
        to listen rhetorically, transformatively, distilling
into words
    spoken words;
I didn't know what they meant at all,
I didn't know who said them:
    They were sounds of anger
                distant anger
        with no special integration. . .
How many people   with pieces of my part
        stand so collectively vague
    lost among some tempers misunderstood in themselves
(too oblique).
My strength fares not yet to fade
with each new revival of close hatred   infectious hatred
        that enlivens me briefly
    leaves me just to a shallow guilt –
                    the way I talk
                norms I chose
            cost of being.
We do not see where others begin,
only where they shall end now.

2

Expanding to tomorrow
the frolics of a sun-lit shadow in a good face
and a habit of forward eyes and honest smell;
retreating each time we relapse
into dangers we conjoin;
accustomed to those expressions
of yesterday
      and those wishes we're through tomorrow;
remembering easiness
in the instrument and glow of uneasy cycles,
I find us together with me –
with the purpose of us –
our words turning inwardly into thoughts.
How language resounds in different forms
and hidden sentiments
and arcana   whispered and those untold
and all kinds of violence
and the resurrection of love
and the dominion of weather
and a tough manner
and rough ideas that sound right
and sex that's too slow in coming
and assumptions to elongate the pain
and pausing people too quick with honor
and an artless land that won't bother
and the touch of this sunrise and sunset land
and the touch of city long streets
and the obsession to get away
and the obsession to stay
and pain that lasts too long to be physical
and a last ascent that can't be recalled
and the loud silence of passion
and the insanity of emotion shaping its theft
and the logic of words
and the destruction of logic by mad words. . .
I'll love us even as I lie

while I meet you tomorrow with all the pleasures
and consequences of yesterday.

3

By pure and sure rite,
I'm used to a pregnant kind of working day,
        as I wash myself again –
                    thinking unusual thoughts,
            brief but cumbersome
in this ageless day I began. . .
Not thinking what I must do in return
        for the persuasive gift of adventure –
getting dressed without thinking what I wear. . .
Naked   barely conscious of public nakedness –
traveling day to day –
making use of direction. . .
Not thinking what I do but what I have done.

To work,
        to take advantage. . .
For sweet looseness   sweet relaxing –
        not much caution in
the tired muscle or nerve that dangles,
        yet uncontrolled;
then, to sleep off a circumstantial rag
                to test mysterious questions
                and questionable mysteries again.

4

The story of home, we know,
as long   mercurial, even massive;
        constant days multiply, only slightly interrupted
        by nascent others and little variety. . .
        To listen for more fable,

more verbs for more spectacle
in the extravagance of one more occasional message.

Addiction to change
holds us disquietly
to be the result, as
we uncover ourselves
to speak once again
of unconscious dreams and unclear places –
with void to correct the false value of specificity.

Emerging old with exaggerated faith
                    in the instinctive wild and hard suave,
we apply a safe measure of confidence,
the will to be slow with affection –
to love slightly but long
and mature with the land.

To invoke ancient myths organized for family cohesion
    and propound familiar thoughts
    and include natural and unnatural notions
of liking and disliking memories we still have of
the power of context to rule a life.

Noting new declaratives from afar –
secure with meager meaning –
grateful for the few truths to be said casually,
we follow principle into paraphrase.

5

I pass old structures
    and old bodies assessing me haunted –
                    the hunger and lies
                    the options
        empty   into strangers more perceptible doubt.

I pass old structures
    and remember other days. . .
I pass other kinds
    and remember others. . .
I remember love taking our time
with patterns of tomorrow
for cathartic passage,
a synonym we have for the future.
I collect tomorrows
    and gather those appearances my face aspires. . .

Our strength is our whims and pieces
bartered away –
attitudes barely molded mold
    every tomorrow with how well today is done in approximation. . .
By tomorrow, we will that much more wend through origin
    and stay bound to everyday's last bounty:

        Conducive smile
        dimple's wrinkle to induce
        sunny amount
        tranquil mean
        or unceasing star.

6

Urban love   apparent love   tremblous love from the street
irreconcilable mind of day   brute confusion
and the knowing of specific unknowing. . .
And we know much more than we shall know.

Moving too fast by faster moving things –
revising with the feral deep and most profound –
finding myself giving way –
    threatening to rely on
        more candid thoughts. . .

Attached to intrepid habits –
     learning by compulsion why I'm thinking of love again –
       insisting upon unrepeatable thoughts
(historically arranged to vertical thoughts),
I bite the acute spontaneity aging on my partial lips –
unconsciously wanting to assume love
on my shy breath
cursive on my searching flesh
that is aware of a home a far home
    a home too far. . .

The mere touch to form an abstract also shone,
        for modern   the details taste too dim
      medicinal   urgent   angular. . .

I have only one life to live,
but I do not live it. . .
I live it by a backward gaze
or with taste hungry for a well-fed future. . .
I do not live it
I do not live it.

7

    Most yearning going back to irrational wish,
   how we would like to turn around inside this life
and vaporously inhale new goals,
          new reason with less erosion. . .
    Anxiety swept away,
   the improved earth drawn nearer. . .

Fresh from lessons of the eloquent earth,
I renew privacy. . .
Love has come,
love has come with dreams
with eyes that can see further with dreams
but can't see just what they see. . .

100

Much further will see the work of several million words working
        that have worked with impatient and inherent greed
        and deposited themselves in solid and less solid shapes. . .

I was once certain, not certain;
as I have taken much,
   I have given much;
it's the law of continuity:
Anything taken must eventually be returned.

All the slow paradoxes
now exist in exiled opinions
that remove me from the land.

Out of the harvest of fastidious and restive ground,
out of cool attention for a mindless cause,
over careful hills protecting the just from unjust idols,
we see the newest towns
       (problems of rich and poor)
adorned   with sad music and bad noise
and the compound problems of compassion;
we prepare roads
for driving design to an estimated range of clarity
and plead to a city emitting romance
played to past pleasures. . .

All stories then slowly created to replace
        the sanctions of true effect. . .

8

I hear diesels
   and the pouring of trucks on highways –
        cars going nowhere somewhere anywhere
     melt into their own lighted speed –
and the screams of hurried invitation
and the wealthy busy with their luxury

and hammers instructing the city
and passionate girls spread before illustrious lights.

My head's curled inside a prominent collar
as smells of fertility recede
wherever land remains shrouded by human ingenuity and stealth. . .
Our people   our people   are starving and boasting –
falling for themselves and calling for others –
caught by glory and humble to the poor –
in love with giving and with greed –
     too old and too young at once. . .
These are my people;
I am one of them.

And the quiet do have the most to say:
For they gather
and think and shuffle
and do not spew
and, most likely, gentle
find gentleness the only toxin to bitterness,
not bitterness,
not even concerned silence
     nor deployed ploy. . .

I've been redeemed from bottom land
and empowered by pines;
harbingering of cities   new cities which I shall always discover,
I've been taken from mud land
and redeemed to best memories
     from good soil   better women. . .
The trees blow straight from steel towers to proud valleys;
I've planned new meanings over the spot;
I've raised new spells over myself and my complexity –
at the point confession most coldly defines
     the distinctions among intellectual games,
as new beliefs give new patience. . .

9

When strength is high and long days are hours,
life is right,
and we feel we will live a little longer. . .
We're alone with fair thoughts,
        conditions are buoyant and suitably tuned. . .
Even our half lies are full.

That we care,
that we wouldn't care   altogether
        but freed enough to want caring
and expect more changes than wishes,
although wishes may be changes already seen.

Learning less about reasons
        but doing more
through prejudicial thunder,
we come ardent,
so that those who die do not remind us of death at all
but prescribe the particulars of the living, and
the more carelessly they die,
more precise the attitudes for our own lives control. . .

As if by prophecy, motives of one generation
become lessons for the next;
        hills do not cover the scars
        nor any beauty will. . .

        We must take hate as hate
                and construct from there;
the valleys, complete with regnant, tumid lies,
        and the white mountains have all been spoken to. . .
        We shall know the hardest verdicts,
for we are hard people   of the hardest conceit. . .
Excitedly thoroughly tomorrow,
we continue that the day will not get much,
        the day will get much longer.

Motion sickness,
>   considerable gestures at nothing   loss of manner
and those unallayed, undiluted memories:
>   The way I held my pose in place
>   leisure smile
>   my worried eyes
>   unmeasured sight. . .
>   The appeal of contrasts
>   has the brightness of advent,
revolution of a notional mind. . .

10

I have seen dust in the city
>   rise for furtive valleys
>   and taking the gains
>   and prevalence of a people
>   and the creation of a natal race
where the essential transcended shall find
>   a native and generous touch
and where wild heretics
will further scuffle with their own abjection
before the aberrant,   but broad ground of tomorrow. . .

>   Magnitude   enslaved again
for the sake of sharing a common community. . .
>   And the grass will grow,
>   and the dust will frame,
and cities will claim,
and an answer will resound in fields with rain
>   beside emancipative roads –
as a city quickly tends the summary of nostalgic comments
>   about the land. . .
Must tenderness always live
by hate or harm to keep itself alive?
And day must still hail its dawn

with the rapid fire of night?
Be more simple;
you know   complexity will work up a frustrated mind.
Have simple dreams:
                    A friend
                 fair luck
                          rough house
                    quiet love
        a good sound of familiar voices
        goodness which is but a familiar voice. . .

            A gleam in a face almost starved
                 shows strain of a terrible virtue, but
                 can it console its own guilty pride?

11

I have supposed midnight spirits
          coming down;
I have been drunk
      or drugged full of rain
      in awe of quick storms;
I have heard baptismal revel from farmers for a hard rain,
and I have cheered wind-fell rain cleaning gutters of a city –
      with rain of the city and long land mixing. . .
I have heard summer crack with a rock message,
          flake of bone life under a dismal sun
      and squeezed of even a night's dampness
              on a prairie that looks over delta gray land.

A city has all its country. . .
              lure and the vegetables they bring
              country people thankful for the city
      haunting the country. . .
              with a foreign levity
      haunting the country. . .
              with the city's maverick power for keeping

haunting a captive country. . .
when the city lays out fresh appetites
for all that's delicious and ripe
haunts this country
and my roads back to genesis. . .
And the memory of a near pleasant trip.

Life has a certain amount of length to it,
and I'm not broken or enough;
I escape chances
out of choice
and fear winning. . .

I was the new revolutionary,
born on the brink of dying
somewhere in an early morning
at some distant place
where places and times do not matter. . .
Sunny women must have laughed
and praised some crying a bit of happiness
at my coming. . .
Congratulations were spread out around a father
somewhere in a young, old city
by votive telegram
that carried me to him for legend's sake.
I came to help
and then disappear –
to help who or what was wounded
or wounded by ill-fated promise;
I took what I was first taught could improve us,
and all the rest were replays.

I threw flamboyant words away,
believing they limited what I meant to say. . .
Then, I talked remarkably and relied on talking:
How I come to others
to be closer to myself.

                    Afterwards,
            I dreamed nothings,
                    and nothing came of them,
            proving how weak dreams are.

12

I was born in the mountains;
I was conceived in the delta.
I got my training in the glory of a top sun,
in mud bottoms dragged surreptitiously
to famous illusion.
I grew between major pine and smaller knolls
and passed away nightly with germinating hints.

A tiny voice rather prospered as a surprising burst
when it loudly expanded my lungs
and the very prime days of exhibition. . .
Uncontrollable flesh crawled eagerly along unreasonable muscle
to anchor grossly solid bones. . .
Mute eyes increased their altitude,
as a modest convex tested unseen motives.
The momentary success of an incipient language
hands suddenly firm
a chest thickly taut
ribs mostly protective
and a face weighing more
released the settling order
. . .Procreation had no reason
to espouse excess.

How much the anonymity of childhood
                    seized me, once
swimming in a state of unpremeditated absence –
catching lightning flies in a jar –
and watching them wilt
(as sleep wrapped more obvious features) –

and lying among new seeded grass –
sleeping near the curbs –
not yet thinking of thought.

13

I came to do something:
To fight pride
        if pride weren't right,
as I was proud or not proud. . .
To beat hope
if hope didn't satisfy the moment;
to take if I were given less;
to take more
if I were given more. . .
To seem strong
if I were very weak;
to tell the truth
if truth were panacean to tell;
to be honest
if I were honest;
to be contrary to established purpose,
if a little.

Yet, the idylls of a solitary and mostly favored player
must be broken, for none can naturally grow endlessly;
origin has but one nature:
To fulfill itself;   unlike the routine for mere occasion,
                it shall not loose swells
of confusion nor the powers of banality
that can foster an intellect's plan,
which, simply for the sake of contrast,
would even alter a better view of contemporaneity. . .
                For without humor or debate,
            the faster crush for the single cause,
                    intemperate of options that perform
                        rarified art or curious flippancy,
                            does not stop its work 'til

sobriety has been spun exhausted to the end of the urge.
And I!   groggy from the ride,
look around to join a faulty penchant
and portion of loneliness
with every tempting freedom of every consciously drifting form. . .
As my craving still dreams libidinous

                                        for unique glimmers
              from involuntary and settled fate:
The shape of my speech
and talents,   the inculcating formality
of conspicuous features –
enlarged toe   maximum ear
and masked correction for primitive conceit.

14

The motive of home descends
upon our world and commands
like a famed specter declaring
its pagan magic and occult possession;
we then learn calls from another side
stop a private attitude of lovers
in their sea of voices remembered,
rejected and returned.

              How the terror of history's increscent field
                    restates for us those odd instructions
we hope will not be retaught again;
for all the ruins of intimate wars
stand as recognition
that nothing is more unrestrained
than the unclear demands of memory.

              In a world without consensus,
home exists only for the compelled,
who attract no siren from foreign, discordant gods
and whose salvation
breathes in mutual approval.

Night Call

I, for one, need no safe exit
out of the wild universe of the midnight cafe,
coffee not much instantly,
rain stuck to shoulders of the storm.

I, for one, know my steps away
warn of solitude, as words hushed
are now repeated in mute resonance;
beer mist, lascivious smoke, loss,

Night calls
gather the loose and dangerous strays
the moral day rejects, so it is said,
but I, for one,
belong to the night, for it and I
refuse the traces and lies of daylight,
and we are one.

EXILE

*"Night Call" was published in **St. Paul's Chapel & Selected Shorter Poems**; Copyright © 2006 by J. Chester Johnson*

Exile

1

Listen to us as you leave;
We're the voice to believe,
The voice to judge your course,
The one to lend recourse.

From us, you will depart
To sort more roads to chart.
Yes, we're the steady voice
To tend a better choice.

Our thoughts follow you there
To see how you will fare,
Adhering to a quaint view,
Leading you to misconstrue.

2

Those who invent shrewd forms
Protect you from the storms –
At least for a little while
'Til you fall for the grand guile.

The phrases will grow hard,
As you remain on guard,
Afraid of what you bring,
Afraid of its dull ring.

But assuming there are dangers,
Learn what you can from strangers –
Some to ply you their own way
And then insist for you to stay.

3

If you go treacherously far,
You must carry an original star,
The thing that shone in this place,
The thing alone to recall the grace.

Don't lose
Before you return.
Don't bruise
Before you discern.

4

Don't entreat
Or be elite;
Stay composed,
Undisclosed.

Listen to yourself moan
That a crowd's on loan.
They come to raise
And land you with praise.

5

You will understand less
In that wilderness,
For beasts tell
Of wealth and oversell.

So, collect the fears,
Correct the years,
Brave the foam
And come home.

6

Stopped between races
While awaiting aces,
You'll feel a cold sigh
For words once held high.

We've seen the hollow treats,
The lost curves, those wise cheats;
Expect a constant appeal,
Ones that would much rather steal.

7

You'll travel many places
And ascend remembered spaces,
But little will be gained
With your flag being stained.

It won't come easy,
When you feel breezy,
When the world you knew
Was the world that flew.

You should have stayed –
Your dues were paid;
And the time you sought
Just can't be caught.

8

Why have it all?
Why take it all?
From too much collection
Comes much indigestion.

So, let it stay there –
The depth and prayer,
The total, the state;
You'll own a fixed fate.

9

Understand it, if you are able:
The unstable follow the unstable.
Avoid thoughtless strands
That foster lower stands.

10

They'll gather your mood
And the way you brood,
The way you learn to point
And how you stay in joint.

Words are cheap
And not very deep
For the restless soul
Of a lone role.

The looks tell degree
But then hide the key;
They stare to please
And laugh to seize.

11

You are not what you thought
Or the correction you wrought.
You are far from the past,
For you simply can't last.

There will be awful times,
Careless sins, perfect crimes.
You shouldn't leer;
Stay here.

12

You will get old
And some less bold,
As the tracts back fade
From the stylish grade.

So, you want a haven
And be some less craven?
Well, while quests may look good,
Stay still with likelihood.

13

Remember what excites you:
The inspiration, the glue.
To respect passion most
Removes a cruel ghost.

Expect the worst:
The things you've cursed,
The ones you've shunned,
The turn that stunned.

Find the first warm hole
And guard its self-control.
Death squads go for such spots
To foil any wayward plots.

14

A story could be told
Of you, a simple mold,
Someone who could not wait,
You who took the bait.

You are the exile –
The one in the aisle?
The one who believes
That the better leaves.

15

Watch the passersby –
They gloat and defy
Or recount their barks
In their great remarks.

Listen first
For the worst;
Choose the best
In the rest.

16

Your opinions will be withheld,
More inhibited then and quelled,
As you carry a fragile pact
To explore and try a new tact.

Name what you want –
Something to flaunt;
Make it so large –
Let a noun charge.

17

You will be missed,
Someone last kissed;
A mark left behind
Does stay on your mind.

Look for familiar parts –
Nothing that merely starts,
Nothing to rudely interfere
With something once so near.

18

It will be fun to escape,
A boon with eyes agape.
But take it more in stride –
Not whole, more for the ride.

Take a step at a time,
If a bit of a climb –
To possess a minor piece
And a much longer lease.

19

It's the ultimate we're talking about,
Conclusions with a marvelous clout –
Nothing to squander or toss,
A game with more lines to cross.

You've a name to declare,
Maybe a legend for a flare.
Say something wise,
Concepts of size.

20

Constraint can also kill,
When you deny the frill
And decide to withdraw
From the pleasure you saw.

So, then, expect doom
And an unempty tomb,
And go easy with the dark,
For it's smart and even stark.

21

Let us hear about the place:
The fun, an instant race.
You don't yet know the test,
But they do eat the guest.

❧

1

Of distractions he was, like most, fully versed;
and, yet, he still knew a carefully arranged touch
is but a transmutation of a desire
to reach for rebirth;   and
what errors he shall commit
make him more dependent on the search.

When a low chorus, emboldened and at hand, trilled in seduction;
when afterwards hid in natural cover, youthful fare, rhymes;
when translucent voices had aired without far-flung echo. . .
Now,

Exile, now nestling in fresh suburban folly, now
surveys awkward oaks survive, survive
thousands of miles, thousands of days from a place
that destines him Exile. . .All he had or could
avail, out of context.

To stay put he heard clearly enough;
the other, less so nominal:
Deconstruct into history to be
what he wasn't, but, for years,
he believed he was meant to be. . .

To do, instead, on his own,
not bound by what he was born,
to reach what could be done. . .Peregrinator.
If it were once broad and general, Exile,
do you lapse to flippancy and maneuver?

Length with its quirks, he ceded,
as Exile greets a glaze rising concordantly over a set of invaded hands;
flesh
      wears
            down and starts to illume
from an excessive rub independent years perform.

What we were guides what we will try,
And what we are will carry pieces of both.

2

Is this what he sought: Calm, pardon,
new contours – to overcome
what one was not given,
                  what was withheld?
to disenjoin to collect all that was left behind. . .

Land, smells,   the houses: Those
                        flavors earning doubtless recall. . .
A chance to be more implied.

Faces   reappear
                        with age hardly inherent;
The face, the faces –   surely, they last;
                of a mixed chorus, determined to resonate and constitute,
                rushing with febrile urge to change, to re-change. . .
He knows too much to survive for long,
as he can find too little
                        of small things of many held. . .

After forty, he'll take fewer notes
                        and rely on code. . .
Don't push too hard – it shows;
and he can't be as ambitious either,
        for that's bad form. . .
        And he should stand flat-footed more often –
to make it look easy, so he's welcomed everywhere.

He, at ageless forty,
began well, but now, well –
those he loved he didn't pursue and those he didn't love
he solicited their support. . .

To amass
less than one shall suppose –
                        best friends become an acquaintance,
                business associates friend –
the world works outside in.

3

Exile looks back in lust
to tour again, even again.
                What consensus events

with crowds, on their feet, raving
for access that could fly. . .
Where an athlete who's never forgetting
and a politician who's not to adjourn protuberant chants –
with congratulations that shorten all doubt.

Collectively, most shift toward commonality,
for there's safety in numbers.   Together,
          they also reminisce in delectable reprise:
Distant pleasures keep memory close.

Stay honest, they say,
                         and manage the promise. . .
Stay near to the one you were
but grow beyond apparency;
nothing's perfect,
they say, as the imperfect speeds toward crisis.
He's the sum of angles he'd like to close. . .

To stop at the liminal trek
                    and accept endurable harvest –
that's the trick: Not to lose a message gained. . .
Gather the essential ascent, a curvature
      that shows no compromise:
One world, at last?

4

Exile probes through another sly glance into fading autumn;
he spies for one transfiguring aside.

In normal times, to be normal requires give and take
and survival on each count.   That's the way
    it shall be: Survival above all else; and
only decayed amusement at the margin.

Those who rely on stories
have reason to travel;
those who can't travel
listen and imagine to take
the trip anyway.

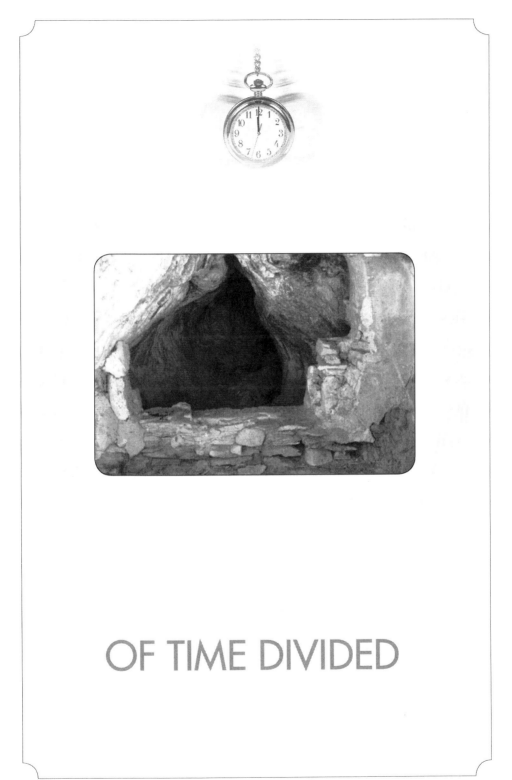

OF TIME DIVIDED

Image copyright: John Vincent Bellezza

Of Time Divided

. . .for he dreaded now that all the dead might
come rushing back through the suction
of that tomb, where the thing had started
writhing, larva-like, out of its stiff reclining –
but then just a simple figure stood there,
crooked in the daylight, and one witnessed:
indiscriminate vague Life accept it.

– from "The Raising Of Lazarus," *The Poetry Of Rilke*
(see Acknowledgments)

A minimal stream of light crept deeper from the mouth of the cave into dissonant and engorged darkness. The light's very narrow shaft framed and confined his fractional meditations, fractional prayers, musings and imaginings, pinched into truncated and abbreviated phrases Lazarus only partially controlled – he, drawn physically to one voice and animation, which led to an ever-widening preponderance of sun and wisdom. Inexorably, burial wrappings fell to the cave's floor, as he bowed and scuffed remarkably toward revelation.

No flare
of nervous light,
no gasp
from fractured air,
daybreak calm,
a running
of smooth water:
Prelusive plain.
Yet, each friend
or scoundrel
is lilting
a refrain
for outbreak
at the accession,
as I awoke –
some to grasp
a hand and irrupt
a language of miracles
for the masterstroke
of inhuman property,
while others
flung themselves
at others nearby
to brand an idiom
among errant words
at the awkward return.
I had been ordinary
and liked it that way.

Should one peer
into that other world,
nothing shall
endure at hand:
New hemisphere;
this new self;
new absence
from things
called real;
familiar face
(instance to an
altered look),
hanging in
a sudden arc and
caught in the re-
evaluation of time.
With something
of such a mark,
can anything past
be so monolithic
again in open air?

I am Lazarus,
someone returned
from a place
no one chose
for a place to be
from which to come.

I am Lazarus,
returning
intact and directional
with a soul pronounced
recovered, having
dimension, volume, fact –
a soul taken to traveling;
memory broke apart,
as I swam through

terse metamorphosis,
and elapsed news
scattered unintelligible
through the heart
of adventure.

You cannot foretell
the time for sleep;
you do not
intend to sleep,
now or later –
something or
someone else
does that for
or against us,
as we infer
it has happened,
for it was
meant to happen. . .
We're more or less
vagaries, acting
how party crashers
are supposed to act;
at such times, times
conflate rapidly, for
we're able to convey
what we'd been,
but that's all past once
something greater than
what we choose decides
casually to choose us.

It's a gamble, you know,
how people turn out.
Some start stout and hot
and leave passion
and industry behind
in an early burn;

then, apart,
in another style,
there are still many
who let slowness
manage any
worthwhile art
they walk
to illume
ever unfolding lives.
I'd done nothing
more to profess
than be born
with a special name,
and there wasn't
anything public
or for acclaim
about the way
I should have died,
but, momentarily,
I turned celebrity,
like a rock star
or fast legend
with ratings above
a simple majority.
People came
to touch and reap
that I, a miracle,
should be.

I am an escapee,
someone to deny
order exists –
upholding free,
urgent texts
for all this that
only a few gain
to display; that is,

to rest on weakness,
to be silly
and inclined
to ridiculous play
with both fault
and fame. . .
So elastic,
less so proscribed;
no sage
nor weatherman –
so unascribed;
to instill fun
for losing everything,
for acquiring
everything else.

Lazarus, I, arise,
I heard it said;
not for nuance
did I prize yet
another day; no,
a share forward
took hold,
and I'd not retreat
from nor qualify
the resurrection –
I'd merely behold
consequences
with promise,
unbound;
I could not stop the
luxurious abyss,
awakening all
I could not contain.

There was no
delicate form, but
empowered theatre,

as storm warranted
upon storm
when death
had been abrogated
by novelty and name;
founding things
to happen
with profound ease,
deliverance gifting
no linear truth.

O Lazarus,
they cried,
as though I
raised myself alone,
master of contrast
and cognitive myth
to which I had
grown for
many and others,
not yet ready
to forsake
more of themselves;
now, you should
not think I,
a trick in time,
transforming illustration,
chose to be blase;
for what are miracles
but an absolute play
on time? How many
voices again slant
their silence
into crowded noise;
once witnesses
to this flagrant –
now, a saint!

What have I learned?
Not much, really –
I can pass beyond myself;
I can make others
believe more and less;
and, if once,
so certain to be
so transcendent,
I eagerly repeat,
at the time,
we shall learn more
than we think we will
from an experience
we cannot forget.

You think margins
and platitudes moved
'cause of it?
Yes and no;
it made a bigger
room taken; magnitudes
caught the flow
as soon as
I was surely gone.
Still, daily patterns
did not modify the way
they occur:
Food tasted likewise –
wine could be both
bitter and sweet,
and getting around town
and failing
to complete directions
chose their usual
dead-ends or rewards. . .
We do what we can
without much of a flair,
no matter how

extraordinary
the affair
drawn – you know,
similar to a dose or two
of first-rate movies
or close liaison,
when we think
they shift everything
inside our
very small histories,
but the suffusive
moment for
an exchange – even
to love and content –
is never quite as fixed
as we prefer.

A conclusion to
array and add
as a fair premise –
that is, one
cannot push one's
own game beyond
the available,
though help may
arrive just in time to
post us beyond this
or that or whatever
else lies fraught
and pat. . .
I learned how
peculiar an act
must be to emend,
and I learned
I could not worry
about the means
to magnify
or suspend

the commonplace,
for either it will come
or it won't, so
stay within
a pendulum's reach
or parenthesis
of realms you know
and try foreign ones
only if you can
depend on
immediate, but
external favor –
that's my motto.

I could like
to forget
even this,
now that
another country
dominates more
of all I do
or want to own,
as one delights in
triumph through
local contrivance –
to rid externality from
the mind has
the romance of freedom.
Though absurd,
we'll fight so
blindly against
the most wonderful
advent or exit
simply for a desire
to dispatch
all we do
at the office or home
or in increment

by our own magic;
the less wont
an occasion, the more
determined a search
for swift freedom.
There's distance in us
that rejects anything
so formidable a gift.

I don't have much time
for this sort of thing –
so, I hope
to get it right
first time around;
for those of us
with more to do
than to contemplate
can't expound,
laboring over open
thoughts while
roaming stasis
with a cleaver;
we take a hard run
at that which works best:
Quick line;
acceptable periods;
favorable verbs;
overt and manifest;
and to fall below
perfection to
keep us modest.

So, let me tell this
with conviction and
speed, and let
life continue
as it is and was.

Everyone predicts
even this life
will end soon
in dearth and loss,
with ache
and cold bodies.
Is it really worth
bountiful content
for us to meet pain
inevitably to follow?
Is it degrees of regulation
or mere conscious
economics?
For pleasure,
I'll always pay
impressive fees;
but to proclaim ecstasy
in place and, there,
still to spin into
depths of the dead,
I'm aware I'll
have to pay
far more than
I plan to pay.

We lose things
by moving on –
to begin a new walk
or to levitate being
above general levels
of brute convention. . .
What we'd lose
for the greater ground,
and for all
we've gained,
there's such
we can't regain.

What one has
has him. . .
For one loves
to take control
of whatever surrounds
the place of heart –
and yet,
what shall be
so close
shall so fully
control the controller.

Lazarus, come forth.
But there are too many
who don't believe
in first occasions;
the old ones, too,
who have seen
too much and
refuse to believe
much more.

At what point
does one decide
to come forth
and be true
to one's calling
and leave the rest
behind? Is it
something we're
able to measure?
Must we rely
on shapes, less shaped,
to give us fare
to form a choice?
In the midst,
the more I find

how little
we direct to outcome –
why the process
proves one can
become what
one can't only
by calling
on regions that allow
what I don't expect.

Lazarus, come forth,
for someone invites me
to stop being normal;
someone must order
things done
and people places. . .
So, Lazarus, I,
came forth,
as an abnormal event
to occur normally,
as something rare
shows more clearly
the reason normal
pieces and patterns exist.

What begins
as an inexplicable feat
will not be reduced
nor made more definite
by an intense effort
to describe
or instruct;
it is merely wonderful,
and it must remain
that way, for
I remember most vividly
the events I can
hardly explain.

So much of a game,
this way and that,
succumbing to boundary,
which matters,
too escapable for words;
so much of the other
we least correct – only
the most agile know
the tricks of the trade. . .
It took more notion
than I could detect
to fancy fun attached
to rhythm and rebirth
for more effect.

Of the appeal
I desire for the things I do:
Why I choose
to go beyond
a safe state,
to explore parts
that have no answer;
why I must become
more than I was
or meant to become. . .
Yet, there remains
this lingering motif
that more is simply
not enough, that
inception can
not spring
forth without
loss of memory
or loss of currency;
one must break molds
and dismiss
acceptable signs
or reliable news;

for whoever can bring
us a new chance
shall first show
scars of loss.

I am Lazarus,
reminder of
the many deaths
one can have,
of every sort,
in and out of love,
with funerals assailing
daily, if not hourly,
for good sport
and even song,
with deaths right and left. . .

Death for want
of something is
everyone's death –
fortune to fortune
to the point of death,
so homespun
and fearsome
as it drives
us inscrutably
toward nothing;
a simple threat
of loss,
so much
a standard death.

But you, Lazarus,
avoiding
singularity of time,
you've finally made it,
cultural hero;
there are fan clubs –

you reveal
sex appeal;
while some flock
to discern you,
others fumble
for an autograph;
and there are women,
who, for glory,
attest to friends,
even if it didn't ensue,
they shared with you
a night of deliberate
and mutual conquest.
It happened mysticly –
you, a scoring star;
people in every city
are soon rushing
to your next tour;
they come, and
some bend their taste
and the angle they infer;
the theatre of rectitude
raised to another grade.

So, Lazarus,
voiding
singularity of time,
you can now tell us:
Has
the still separate world
made this one
a little less apart?

MEDITATIONS
ON
CIVIL RIGHTS ACTIVISTS

...history trembled before them

Image courtesy of Trinity Wall Street; artwork by Marc Tremitiere

Meditations On Civil Rights Activists

. . .history trembled before them

Jonathan Daniels

I am Jonathan Daniels, Dear Lord.
You know me by name and shattered flesh.
I do not mind the bullet-wide holes,
For into torn places the good breath
Of the Holy Spirit has come and
Played, replacing with joy my pain and death.

To the ground, Ruby Sales, enough is
Enough – you shall be safe to begin
Anew, a life before you and free,
A life wrought of choice and space –
You, to forgive all to a greater love
Of all; for lives raised is life praised.

Do not grieve for me, Ruby Sales, for
Sweet Jesus has borne my wounds home – and
The blood of my body, the blood of
Medgar, Martin, the Philadelphia three,
And all the rest have soaked the soil
And the soul and saved the South and me.

W.E.B. Du Bois

I am Du Bois, Dear Lord.
Here I lie to die today in Accra, Ghana,
My home, but not my home,
One day before the March on Washington, August 28, 1963 –
A day, a turning point to be,
And I shall not see.
O God, take me to that home briefly –
Just for a glimpse of the yet to be.

I am prized, I am recognized
By heads of state – and shuttered by the country of my birth,
But for my mind.

Have I lived too much in the mind?
What did I do with this abundant head that rocked with thoughts
Never ending? I question myself. . .
The mind, all our minds that were to free us in a country of blood,
Our black blood
Spilling over streets of hatred, a mammoth flood.

I thought and thought and talked and talked and wrote and wrote,
And, yet, my kindred died –
In the Atlanta murders of 1906, where I lived and cried,
Or by the hundreds in the Arkansas pogrom
(1919, wasn't it?) that my poet, Weldon, decried to be The Red Summer.

My mind running uphill always,
Challenging the path, gaining strength against resisting forces,
Never stopping – the brain used as a battering ram
For justice and freedom. . .sometimes, near explosion –
So it felt – it would not stop, ever flowing with reason and reasons,
Asleep or awake, the pounding of the waves
For the cause never-ending, always clinging.

Even now, at death's window, I visualize, and my wish to foresee too much
Shall terrorize these final moments.

How I pray just for one day more and half a world away –
To be at the nexus.
They say I helped.

A heart does not open without instructions from the mind –
That is true, O Lord, isn't it?
Once, I knew, for sure.
I now believe there are limits to the mind,
And still, in that brutal place,
Only through the pace of the mind did we move uphill.
Curious, isn't it? We had to be superior to be equal.
Even now, who's like King?
Who can match him in courage, thought, and sting? –
As he simply asks to sit where they sit, eat where they eat,
Learn where they learn.

It is time for others,
Who sing and reach across lines with open hearts
And the love for one nation, one people, one springtime.
Maybe, the heart has heard the mind.
Maybe, I am the mind that told them so.

James Weldon Johnson

I am James Weldon Johnson, Dear Lord.
I am a maker of songs,
I am a teller of wrongs;
A singer of harmed souls
   And dread sins,
A singer of coldest holes
   And wiser wins.

But not for the glorious and famous
Do I scribe these lines of lost tears and years,
But for the worn and tired, the black and torn,
Who'll wait no longer for their freer fate.

O, my people of this land, sing with me
The bold songs that shall wake
The faint and falling,
Sing with me a nation's humanity,
Sing of the country's indignity,
Sing for a nation's symmetry
And of the country's infidelity.

Sing songs of prejudice
And a song of justice;
Sing jubilee,
Sing free.

Sing of past agony,
Sing of last bigotry,
And sing anthems of the country's tragedy.

We shall sing until we're louder than blood,
Until all hate fails, wrecked in the Red Sea's mud.
We shall sing until acts of pain then drown,
And, as Joshua's blast broke Jericho's crown,
Until the walls of race come tumbling down,
Down, down, down. . .

Ida B. Wells-Barnett

I am Ida B. Wells   Dear Lord
With Mississippi of my first days   Memphis of my noisy days
And Chicago of my fabled ways.
I don't apologize   rarely ask for forgiveness
And prize pistols and rifles for black folk to meet
The guns of white devils   for resistance can beat the halfhearted.
By learning to stand on my own two feet long ago   I spoke my mind loud
And clear   and spoke it well   if I do say so   surely suing
The railroad when only 22 in 1884   for treating me poorly.
I later covered firsthand the race massacre of Elaine Arkansas
Daring bullets and knives galore without a scratch.
I'd see every inch straight on without amendment
Since justice is justice Lord   and I'd not flinch.

I withstood wild yellow fever
Though my good parents and sibling were vanquished
So don't tell me to slow down   I've seen those who utter only "yes"
They're the first to go   and go badly. All
Agree I'm a most public person   a Joan of Arc against the lynching day
Yet I've learned to argue that everything   absolutely everything
We do is private. So why this lynching and me? While I hate mad dogs
As we quickly must sense traits of a mad dog   and I'll tell
Spiritless shameless mad dogs'll tear and rip alike 'til nothing remains
Still to savage more. Lynching is always like that.
But I'm one to catch a mad dog midair
And I'll do all I can to stare one down
Even if it looks like a lion in full gallop.

So I'll tell you the excuse for lynching
Continued in use   most thirsty hell   the violation of white women by
Black men. But witnessing enough rape and compulsion then
Sanctuary suspended   we know black women had far more
To complain about from white men than white women had to complain
About from black men   and yet and yet. What else did I teach
O Lord?   The blessed won the rope and bullet without cuts to bone

Or brute mutilation   the less blessed were canned in barrels with nails
Driven in   every side and rolled down long vales   or were   to disgrace
Ignited after branded face to feet   searing irons melting away all flesh
That it's impossible to call the limits of cruelty
For the exceptional demons took teeth hair and bone
As trophies for white children or first cousins to share.

O Lord   somebody had to tell the story
And I did   when I told myself ages ago
I write what I think   with consequences uncajoled
For those of us only like that   it's no
Surprise   we are what we have to see.

Yes   I told the world about lynching   as
One could not digress with one word in excess
"Lynch"   a razor in the throat
A stone in the chest   a spike forever
To a decent head and better heart.

Martin Luther King, Jr.

. . .Martin, the truth is pointing: You laid waste
        A pride of artifice and taste
                And changed our language of memory.

But the message you left behind
The world has yet to find. . .

      Few could fathom
      the tremors of change prevailing
      alongside games and
      the consequences of one faithful irony:
      For God shall slowly bless
      those who are given less.

Let the promise go ahead,
And we will follow instead,
As martyrs sought a perch
To illuminate the search.

      For time on end:
      We couldn't rescind the lie that made us weak;
      we couldn't speak naturally;
      we couldn't hear the white-robed lessons of the night;
      and we turned to a wrongful fear. . .
      It's maddening the promises we edit to keep a bad habit.

So, we went away to think awhile –
Thoughts kept private became our style.
Many wanted to do a lot more
That traditions worked to ignore.

      You, meting the difference between what we were
      and what we professed to be –
      and what we were was better.

Some didn't care for the gist, when you spoke subtlety poetically. . .
To assume we were better –
now, that's truly revolting and revolutionary.

Black, white and all the rest
Would be asked for their best –
To slant new codes through one boundless test
And for atonement, a mighty protest.

It was convention tossed
the way you went into places
you didn't belong, where you'd be lost;
we closed our eyes and watched the evening news.
                    Hardly undone,
you chose to check how strong the heart of malady.

Some were moved,
Some removed.
Others would leave
What some still believe.

The mind racked, and unleashed terror surged the brain;
                    the attacks were rending;
            for whoever must deny fear feels it most,
and, Martin, you of all were to defy
close effects to reveal it could be done
so others shall prefer The Great Liberation. . .
And they did, and you did.

A louder brute groped about,
But we questioned how stout,
Even as the white bull faces
Put blacks through their paces.

Was the real message then, Martin: Submission to fear
                distorts all things, corrupts all wills,
corrodes all loves, kills off the first and instant motives
we yearn to proclaim? Was this the infinite intent?. . .

160

For we came to know words weren't the whole event.

You took it upon yourself
To rid yourself of self;
A rite action of a strong hand
That works for the good, not the grand.

Martin, there's less contrast, and rare lights pale;
without fire, the best soon lie stale, hot breaths hang limp,
muscles atrophy. We're ready to be lit,
but the pulpit stands empty, and sundry veer,
hearing popular and pleasing
voices singing sweetly elsewhere
that much less, oh, much less, conveys a much easier, quieter finesse.

You measured things by intent
To know what others really meant
And did not trust the law
Or how it could seesaw.

A phalanx of angry racists
        raced through the hectic wound
                that couldn't match you, Martin, when the bullet split
flesh from vowels. They rushed in
                to collect spoils, a storehouse of colossus
        and message that carried a generation
of both courage and advent, and to steal away
across Memphis to sequester the victor's remains.
Silence fell over the struggle,
and lessons sighed enough was enough.

Which way you went
Meant the word you sent.
Wisdom you infused
Could not be refused.

Martin,
you wouldn't let the dead stay dead;

for they had a purpose: To show an array
of reasons the past should pass away.
And, yet, so, we will learn once again:
Whoever kills the past it must also kill.

...Let Justice
Roll Down Like Waters
And Righteousness
Like A Mighty Stream.

—Amos

MARTIN

Martin

Dedication

To my students, who attended the African-American Drew School in Monticello, Arkansas during 1969–70, the year before full racial integration was mandated for the town's public education system. Constructed by the local African-American community partially out of vacated medical buildings and barracks from an abandoned World War II prisoner of war camp, which had been located on the outskirts of town, Drew, bearing colors of blue and gold and a sports moniker of "The Lions" and employing strikingly limited resources, educated the town's African-American children. Once schools in Monticello were completely integrated, Drew ceased to exist.

. . .Martin, the truth is pointing: You laid waste
a pride of artifice and taste
and changed our language of memory.

But the message you left behind
The world has yet to find. . .

Few could fathom
the tremors of change prevailing
alongside games and
the consequences of one faithful irony:
For God shall slowly bless
those who are given less.

Let the promise go ahead,
And we will follow instead,
As martyrs sought a perch
To illuminate the search.

For time on end:
We couldn't rescind the lie that made us weak;
we couldn't speak naturally;
we couldn't hear the white-robed lessons of the night;
and we turned to a wrongful fear. . .
It's maddening the promises we edit to keep a bad habit.

So, we went away to think awhile –
Thoughts kept private became our style.
Many wanted to do a lot more
That traditions worked to ignore.

You, meting the difference between what we were
and what we professed to be –
and what we were was better.
Some didn't care for the gist, when you spoke subtlety poetically. . .
To assume we were better –
now, that's truly revolting and revolutionary.

Black, white and all the rest
Would be asked for their best –
To slant new codes through one boundless test
And for atonement, a mighty protest.

Some learning faster than they concede,
            as many who can't learn
                stand proud to the gadding fault. . .
So, Martin, you roiled up slow learners, daring
them to be the minimalists time said they had to be.

It was convention tossed
the way you went into places
you didn't belong, where you'd be lost;
we closed our eyes and watched the evening news.
                Hardly undone,
    you chose to check how strong the heart of malady.

Some were moved,
Some removed.
Others would leave
What some still believe.

                No one's apt to understand
                weakness quite as well as the weak,
        panicked at the onslaught of transition. . .
    While you, encumbering pavid spots with the weak clamoring
    to incite its staggered ranks. . .And while you, in turn,
                    to isolate lesser sorts
        until they sat alone, dull and anachronistic. . .

You expected too much
From those in a clutch,
Who coaxed words inside
And found which ones had lied.

    Rampant rumors to contort and control
    the elusive you,

un-American, philistine, confusionist!
All names confecting to exaggerated form. . .

The episodes caused much drama,
As they threatened further trauma.

In the bright light of exposure,
The choices, long and pure;
But gray motives failed in the age;
For they flagged in an ancient cage.

Does little risk make one free? Even a gradient to pause?
You'd spot another withering,
            who laid low with treasures and stillness,
                who'd wait for an attack to pass. . .

The pay, not much for the work –
Breaking molds received no perk.
A martyr's wound shall leave lofty stars,
But ferocious jobs gather no tempting scars.

You astonished history
                and put it into remission;
more was possible heightened the theme.

Claiming here and now, you, not the guise
to be dismissed as fictional or transient, but
to go into cloisters where anger burned white.

You measured things by intent
To know what others really meant
And did not trust the law
Or how it could seesaw.

And who was neither as surly nor angry
as the great divide implied? . . .Yet,
those still damned to fall, murdered by night,
bombed anyway or swept away;

          old phrases blustered; for
     they'd not fight on your limpid ground
     nor by your votive terms. . .

Martin, so you were led by the dead
And wouldn't rely on what one said;
And some were sure you'd quit,
While others offered you the bit.

     Could you really see another side up a mountaintop?
     Or was it just for magic? What else did you concoct to entice?
              An uncontrollable taste
     with no precedent to swallow?
     No wonder judgments broke out; for you offered no finale,
     giving intellectual hounds feasts of theory,
     food for those who merely bark speedily. . .
     With no refined order, while protectors hectored to distraction. . .

         You left more to chance
     and those codified more than a little mystified.

And viral names – how bad?
Not for any quaint fad.
You took us as we came
And treated all the same.

     Then, a fixed polemic
         with both sides winding
              you down in lore. . .   To one,
     you hid illusions you wanted by stealth,
              and to the other,
     a precipitant light under dark moons
     for exercise and sunrise.

The ease you'd show
At then saying "No"
Disguised the lonely times
You'd find from faithless crimes.

We relied on early reads when we followed at hand
         the swell over the land,
when you directed an outcome
that couldn't be stopped. . .

How did you stay on target,
So you controlled the market?
Most of us get lazy and tired
And wish we had not been hired.

    As the past shaped us
    to haunt the present. . .One man
    will configure, too, the metamorphoses once he decides
        they shall exist
    and then serves them fresh to bring us 'round. . .
            Martin,   nemesis to the mad-dance
                        at a traditionalist's ball.

You caught waves at the crest,
And we now know the rest;
You never did turn back
Or slow to hide in the pack.

2

    The movement's allayed –
        yes, slipping a bit. . .
    Most still believe, so they say,
    which hardly lifts to instill;
    for only small numbers ever erupt to outland. . .

    And it will now and after go forward
        in spurts and starts and stomps and taunts,
    and on it goes. . .
    We need teachers but hear whispers instead,
    so we languish
    in a dappled message, in half secrets again.

You could not wait on those
Who knew no highs, all lows.
You ran only with a few or alone
To curious realms to which you were prone.

A tepid May
then, well, took your place.
Folks got groggy,
others coy.   And for hordes far beyond home,
you flared a mere moment,
as many dismissed most virtue,
blaming fragments from a corrupt age, and
plotted games with an end in mind.

You wore the weight,
You shed the hate;
You've had some fun
And widely won.

It's laziness too deep to fight,
while we drift through extra strophes and clefts.
Oh, there's progress: Jobs held,
houses occupied – with us
short on effort. . . The reminiscent words
interrupt sleep or dinner or our spicy epigrams
or making love or using love
or taming money or saving the next big trip
to purgative flats.
Elaborating on a trendless road,
we chase another pitched voice somewhere dim.

A blade sunk into your chest –
A surprise cut through your quest;
All things poised put off guard,
The dread of reprise unbarred.

Once stigmata dug into simple remains
of the testament,   each scar

with its individual telling
　　　　　a safeless sermon. . .
The loss said, a greater glory!
And when one persuasive scar, now collected, shall wait unhidden.

The ambits were considered sad
With lots of the land gone mad;
For fuss about a certain war
Caused much for many to abhor.

A louder brute groped about,
But we questioned how stout,
Even as the white bull faces
Put blacks through their paces.

　　　Politics so aping theatre, we all construe;
　　　　　　　and a wild complexion abounded
　　　　　once the bullet pierced fugitive space.
　　　Time moved away from the movement.　Oh,
　　　　　many a trace we still recant; for
　　　some think twice now before ruinous words,
　　　and we're probably then additionally civil,
　　　　　　　but by how much? –
　　　with voluble nods leaning toward a just task
　　　to hide too often an awkward mask.

You took it upon yourself
To rid yourself of self;
A rite action of a strong hand
That works for the good, not the grand.

　　　It's likely ennui
　　　would have happened anyway –
　　　　　　　　　the price raised, more the chore;
　　　　　and once technology amassed
　　　its shadowing text
　　　and loosed its indomitable sway. . .

Recast, recess, and revision gaining hold
            with less chance for verse to traverse;
hoarding to have any one had.

There was enough blame to go around;
About those harmed, guilt stuck tightly wound.
In harm's shade, neither the hand
Nor the hurt rose above reprimand.

3

Martin, there's less contrast, and rare lights pale;
    without fire, the best soon lie stale, hot breaths hang limp,
            muscles atrophy. We're ready to be lit,
    but the pulpit stands empty, and sundry veer,
            hearing popular and pleasing
    voices singing sweetly elsewhere
    that much less, oh, much less, conveys a much easier, quieter finesse.

You waited on no one
And had picked up the run.
Those who have something to catch
Shall cause a country to stretch.

    Somewhere down in that vein
    to yield currency
            could sprout a lust of disgust
        for those whom you fought to mend.
    How you displaced distaste
    with elusive grace,
                though it could have vaunted another route –
        with those talents stirred
    toward blood spring –
    with spirit's disguise hanging vulpine for antagonists
    you came to amend.   Only a few, a very few,
                    actually joined that army of turns,
            but more, many more fell into the prodigious thought

we knew should be preferred for the good
of even those who mostly demurred.

In our age, we'd matured fast,
As though divided by caste;
Opposing, type against type;
Differences pruned so ripe.

    A contrast between what you
    wished and how you wished for it,
    when style and complaint played one
    another off without being awry. . .   And to turn
    to a laugh to turn more into more and many,
    and to turn those untouched,
    you turned to lyrics again and to Godhead songs
    for many and more turning to get there.

Danger resides at the light,
Where cold myths fall in full blight,
Where bad rules decompose for space,
And rule breakers set a fierce pace.

    More fun, less drear,
        the demoting of golden calves
           and molding them miniature. . . It's dawn
    the way a laugh undoes tradition; for if we
    dream grave, a foe constructs
        its yawn; those grim sorts inspire none
           nor have any length,
    but humor carries the sun beyond midnight,
    as we're borne to flirting, urgent wit.
    Be fleet, but firm; laugh and be wise.   That's
    high management style.

You sang, Child of God, a saving figure
(Someone whom we would have to injure)
Into depths where you weren't supposed to go
For justice the world could not bestow.

Upon an unending field on which to work, Martin, you plowed;
if one shall choose to labor over another's soul,
            the project never ends. . .
Unlike chairman of the board
or coach of the year. . .
Souls insist on lingering beyond rank
            or chronology. . .
When one fiddles
in souls with no sign-up sheets
            or clocks or whistles to raise
            or end a day,   what skills convince?
Some deem failure; others – hope, gravitas;
still others favor vigilance or a tinge of the brute;
devotion to an enduring fruit. . .

With the Church indeliberately needed,
With indictments then constantly heated,
You counted on harder than glinting words
To halt the hotter gallop of coarse herds.

            Divining the verse before you loosed a line or two,
            keener than we were thinking. . .Then, there began
            a supple joining of joys few observe
                  but, at last, would liberate. . .
            The Old Testament rousing a lyrical ascent,
                  we waited for someone
               to conjoin justice with anthems; you,
               relying on uncommon art
               for a common start. . .

You stuck to your guns,
Not like mannered sons;
You bled and also wept
And sometimes overslept.

            It took someone so near to settle your muteless space,
                  to share alliances to assure or rebuke. . .

Elevated behavior for imbuing?
Close eloquence hiding beheld.
They, who could still cringe in place
at the places you placed yourself. . .
Whose for help?   What apostles?. . .
As they seek or do or seek to do. . .
I'm talking of those whom you wanted, Martin,
for candor and reason,
when you were alone with devilish rain
and sample plague or the doggish dark. . .
Ones who mattered still
after efforts fell to grace. . .
Ones who willingly stood by
and waited for the cast to leave, ones who sensed
wisps calming in the sum
of peril and compulsion. . .
Ones not to trick or undermine;
for were you lost once they lost you?
Who?
No, not those
who sought too much, but those
who forgave
you weren't what you seem. . .
Those who vowed you
can't be a leader always; for a leader's
true only when racing how
to follow,
pacing the heights
by which one drove further putative and general.
Those who love cannot
love by adopting
quirks that merely make them unusual. . .
When taking advice,
one's neither first
nor last. . .

4

And weighed by weak rewards,
Inflicted by ponderous guards,
Impounded in crowded jails –
Shortly, our faith in pain pales?

We had much refusal to recall:
A raided zeal, a collective stall;
A history, here, just all too mean;
Will a single ounce finally be made clean?

How did you not shove or nudge
the lonely mass
into a small corner, useless cranny,
a latch to close and lock,
        until the boards popped open,
    and   bilious fever   and palpitant wounds   spewed   through
the system,   pushing   through
        glands and pores,   and on out into the street
and the world beyond?

The mind racked, and unleashed terror surged the brain;
                    the attacks were rending;
            for whoever must deny fear feels it most,
and, Martin, you of all were to defy
close effects to reveal it could be done
so others shall prefer The Great Liberation. . .
And they did, and you did.

Was the real message then, Martin: Submission to fear
            distorts all things, corrupts all wills,
corrodes all loves, kills off the first and instant motives
we yearn to proclaim? Was this the infinite intent?. . .
For we came to know words weren't the whole event.

A calm congruity goes far
Where the tough and loving are –
With the wealth of laws ever unfair,
Their next victim still everywhere.

Behind walls,
incarcerated light, Martin,
where, in turn, you once again emblaze, as
the pumping and pressing of inevitability reigned.
All wait to watch
bars of the jail melt into soil and
something fructive and level take root
and spread across the realm.

For the longest march,
mightier performance, you,
rising
to eloquence until even faint politicians
chose to intervene; many a witness there were
to the impressive riot of the heart –
inside gray tombs meant for death and dismemberment. . .
Juxtaposition,
that's what does it: The drab and derelict
extruded into design and dash,
and the mixture bears this uncontrollable clench. . .
In juxtaposition,
laws no longer view themselves as full-time
and repel back from the consumptive
roar of pride. . .
You, unchained!

Freest interludes simply couldn't congeal or last;
For those who grift the future held you to the past.
But you'd learned the stuff of physics calling still:
Whoever kills the past it must also kill.

The subject lured fire
you knew how to use. . .
                                    And the social repair did not inhabit
                                    a string of sterile halls
nor garrets occupied
by cool stoics or icy moles. . .
                                    No, you brought it crossroads
                              and flared it more classic
than an Alabama song
or hometown weekend.

A phalanx of angry racists
            raced through the hectic wound
                    that couldn't match you, Martin, when the bullet split
flesh from vowels. They rushed in
                to collect spoils, a storehouse of colossus
            and message that carried a generation
of both courage and advent, and to steal away
across Memphis to sequester the victor's remains.
Silence fell over the struggle,
and lessons sighed enough was enough.

Which way you went
Meant the word you sent.
Wisdom you infused
Could not be refused.

        Martin, you wouldn't let the dead stay dead;
        for they had a purpose: To show an array
        of reasons the past should pass away.
        And, yet, so, we will learn once again:
        Whoever kills the past it must also kill.

Dietrich Bonhoeffer
(February 4, 1906 – April 9, 1945)

FOR CONDUCT
AND INNOCENTS

DRAMA IN VERSE

For Conduct And Innocents

Drama In Verse

Born 1906 in Breslau, Germany into a prominent, but not especially religious family, Dietrich Bonhoeffer embraced the teachings of Protestantism early, becoming a well-known theologian and acclaimed writer while still in his twenties. When most of the Church leadership in Germany crumbled under the weight of Nazism, Bonhoeffer and a group of colleagues set about establishing the Confessing Church as a moral and spiritual counterforce. During a sojourn away from Germany in 1939 to teach at Union Theological Seminary in New York City, Bonhoeffer determined that in order to earn the right to shape the future of his country, he was compelled to go back to Germany and work for the removal of Hitler and the regime. Upon his return, ironically employed as an agent of the German military intelligence office, he became engaged in numerous anti-government activities that included supplying of assistance to Jews and creating a network, both inside and outside Germany, of clergy and others who sought peace. Bonhoeffer also plotted with a group of co-conspirators to overthrow Hitler; toward that end, he participated in organizing efforts to assassinate the Nazi leader. Arrested in April, 1943, Bonhoeffer remained in prison for the rest of his life. Remnants of the Hitler command were so obsessed with Bonhoeffer's death that they executed him at the Flossenburg concentration camp, located near the Czechoslovakian border, on April 9, 1945, only two weeks before American liberation of the camp. Stripped of clothing, tortured and led naked to the gallows yard, he was then hanged from a tree.

❦

Author's Comments

For Conduct And Innocents covers a time frame, directed by major events in German history during the period, 1940–43, which preceded Dietrich Bonhoeffer's arrest. The conversations within *For Conduct And Innocents* are, of course, fictionalized; however, Bonhoeffer's presence in the particular locations at the particular times, when discourse occurs in this drama in verse, is derived from historical accounts. For this composition, I found it necessary to invoke liberties for certain characters. As an example, Dietrich Bonhoeffer was one month shy of his thirty-seventh birthday and Maria von Wedemeyer only eighteen at the time of their engagement in January, 1943; accounting for these facts, I simply could not fathom a dialogue between Bonhoeffer and a teenage woman, during the crucial period prior to the theologian's arrest, encompassing the subjects and issues explored in *For Conduct And Innocents.* He had something to say about this intrinsic problem himself a number of months after the betrothal, voicing a wish that he could speak to her about his personal, theological thoughts and concerns. Apparently, later in life, Maria also spoke of her own misgivings about the effects of her young age at the time of engagement to Bonhoeffer. Readers can observe I have made adjustments to actual history, to wit, a new fiancée, Gertrude— conceptually, a bit older than Maria—was created. In addition, for the part of Richard N., there is no one individual on whom the role is based, but rather, it embodies a collage of persons intensely connected to Bonhoeffer's goals and labors at the time. I trust readers will forgive these accommodations and understand the usefulness of the latitude taken.

For Conduct And Innocents contains a version of the verse composition form, elastic rhyme. A discussion of the pattern, as practiced in this piece, appears in the general Author Comments at the beginning of this book.

For Conduct And Innocents

Characters

Dietrich   - *German Theologian and Nazi Foe*

Gertrude   - *Dietrich's Fiancée*

Richard N.   - *Dietrich's Colleague and Friend*

Voices of the Condemned   - *Voices ad seriatim*

Opening

Voice of the Condemned, #659537:

Small amounts of love contain a modest gift, but the
Larger parts of love speak prophecy. After all, we accept
Nothing gains quite without mystery, closely unbound, untamed.
The thoughts to convey – the unfurling effects of mystery; we're
Daily solving to relay in our own peculiar way the
Undisclosed lure of unexplained times.
                                    But, at this place, all order lies
In an irreverent call that we're destined some fake charm
For a magical ride that shall alter the canons of cruelty
For a thousand years and where extraordinary delusion sits
Comfortably and damnable. . .
As blunt, desperate attempts to mock crudely the mystery again
Gather. . .as a wayward excuse to justify the narrow, too
Narrow, forms. . .as the man-gods, swiftly loose, start to work
Miracles to induce a desire to be remade.
                            And here, enough safe logic rounds to
Murder with ease and texture; and now, inhumane, the quicker
So many trivialize the unknown and unknowable. . .

In 1940, Dietrich Bonhoeffer joins Abwehr, the German Military Intelligence Office, where his brother-in-law, Hans von Dohnanyi, is already employed; Abwehr would later be seen as an organization with an element of officers that planned and worked for the downfall of the Nazi regime. Indicative of Nazi cynicism in the justification of aggressive military exploits are the airborne invasion of Holland and the campaign into Belgium, both of which occur in May, 1940 and are defended by Hitler and his party as being necessary in order to safeguard the neutrality of both countries. Later in the year, Germany conducts a major bombing operation against London, the most fierce air attack on a city in history, up to that time.

Act I
September, 1940
Location: Klein-Krossin Estate
Near Kieckow, Germany

Richard N.:

Blame the cold, for it takes the winter's loss better
Than we can in our short and loosely controlled wit. . .
Tolerating these regrettable times. Our own lesser rules turning aside
And, in blood, mutating into those outside the approved decrees. . .
                                        Transgressions laying claim to what
Appears normal flood to fill an empty
And grim face. . .

Dietrich:

The sentenced, Brother K, more excessive, searched for his life again –
Seeing his death as the last, best chore, as the freedom
To live. . .So, he waited there just to be caught,
A victim who doesn't command an alternative.

Gertrude:

Still, I can
Understand a man who falls openly – the desire to
Contain this life in a context or brand becomes too
Haunting. Both fate and death, equal weights of the end?

Their bodies creak they were so right. No one dares
Stop them, for it should last like a minor, bleak
Burst, or, to be laid aside, in a lost time
Left. And he was taken away lame, not like a blasphemed
Thug, and, of course, he would return after the garbled
Phase of taut hysteria ran down.

Dietrich:

Then, he had, above trite plays,
Never supposed to vie in absurdity. Did his blinking smile
Reflect a larger laugh inside a higher view? To consider a
Moment, unhinged, of lonely principle – not in a little while,
He would be undone by the tracks of a false country.
He called
My ways too serious – that I don't rely on others
While I yearn: 'You take them like a free lunch,
And you're always full of conditions for your own sake,
Even without working at it. Since you try that little
Game to be perfect, there's no doubt you've then learned
No trick to keep from loving yourself mostly and the
Nature of your own thoughts, too steep for general use. . .'

Would a day of tragedy and violent designs suit
As his best day?. . .
He would hear and think something like witchcraft
Had taken hold of murmurs. . .and a curse and the
Sheer fulfillment of an omen no longer implied any surprise.
No calculus rewarded him, when he would comment:
'We cannot stop the worst assault – late, early, but

Too many will now have to swap their strident, cruel play
For damnation. Nothing simple finally can remain simple, if too
Simple. . .As dissolution adds a common touch to us all.'
                              That his own classic
Cures are gone, I drift away from the present like
Mist, for no one halts this marauding and public shift. Now
Tossed into the clutch of contrast, I feel too natural
To be envied, too bound and unembossed to be remembered.
                              Brother K, that questioner of
Habits, decided to plumb and forge my
Faith into aloof studies of trouble, his saying at the
Time, 'Final conclusion is an unbridled animal,' a forming proof
That it couldn't be checked, cornered or incarcerated. The problem
Remained theory; God was also theory. Once aimed, we worried
Him away and hoped him back again. . .
                              Thus, he fell
Without friends, like a raven or hawk, without array, split
Into naught by a vote of currency's intent. There, his
Own personal dramas left him, but, by the stanzas he sought
For his own demise, a name and outline he knew
By heart and proclamation.

                    They did not incise beneath
To emphasize him, though he had saved many from confusion
On occasions by his wise and irrefutable wait mostly
And very slow logic; they did not even care to retell
The times he freed them from obvious and thick pain.

And now, his patience counted as a reason some practice
A cold and general noise and vow to savagery against
The narrow and private prayers he retained. The strain to
Forget fell on their lies, breathing secondhand whispers as though
Their secrets could hear. . .the moment speaking clearly enough to
Show the purveyors had more power, but debts than they had
Even dreamed.

Gertrude:

Two opposites converge so neatly, though they don't long endure
Side by side. Imagine functional ones to emerge among
The religious, and you, us, the most naïve and sacred,
Imagine the two of us, so clamorous, impolitic in program
And thought.

Dietrich:

We seem in no shape to be any less
Detached than we were. God's not so far
Away, at our hands and traffic, from the quotidian and
Smallest cell, arranged to be the per se and the circle.

They've tried to ruin the face of God, now further
Behind, to set fear without mercy. As God cannot
Choose to desert even the maniac, as I remind myself
A friend was chained into the laws of usual men,
We know we abide a broken Eden and ordained risks.

Richard N.:

                                                    You stand one
Unknown away from the next devolving crime, where, though as
A spy in a lier's shirt, you would be expected
To try at all times to choose an alibi or
The side that always wins. . .They take you as seriously
As you sometimes take yourself. . .

                              Should we
Decide you're too similar to the opaque and thunderous nun
Whose dress rattled crisp and unwrinkled, whose straight and undivided
Mission shall be no warmer than the flavorless
Precision of your good logic?
                                        Even now, we adopt our

Counterpose and behavior this readily, mere frank brothers who withstood
The short surge and fight over who would be the
Truest, for only one vision can purge and rule the
Resistance. Yet, do we say we are their opposites, so much
Like the way children will, at times, set their mouths
And unroll, pretending to be strangers?
                              Or can we, for fact, relay that
We're capable of beating them strength against strength, goal against
Goal? – To rewind our own sheer rigidity to put ourselves
At peace?. . .
                    No one believes the heretics can be used, but you
Have done it. They'll swear you misled the best, and
They'll hate you the worse for it – you, who took
Your own principles even more completely against the perverse roar –
                              another blunt move into arrogance;
And they'll sharply despise the arrogance dumbly and declare a
Toxic and infernal war more devotedly. . .

You handle their power as their weakness, like
A fanatic handles a one-liner to herald for himself
Those appealing qualities of genius. They, like alchemists, first hoax
Many with the specter of glory without degrees and then
Describe and leave the rest of a nature nourishing mere
Homage – that fated tide madly we've felt of the decline
Is all that's left.

Gertrude:

            If love could carry freedom from
Place to place, I'd try the deft step to make
It freest among leaders. I'd tap into your order
Long before you can recognize it as fresh, so young
In a passage resting upon your simplicity for
Strength. You needed so little pilgrimage from someone there
Who just listened.
                    You carry that certain scent of death
In a subject, Dietrich; you, to measure robust killers touting

Too much low ambition. . .
                              And you plan to rule and
Expose fault to clarity, knowing the touch of obscure parts
Should again vanish quicker than sound. Yet, you came then
As a stranger – I now wish you could have stayed
That way. . .
                    I understand you look to evade and defeat
Death through another death, for you're heroic enough to command
And conceive that your form of promoting eclipse does exceed
The advantage of theirs. . .that a naïve world shall swallow
Another taste. . .
                        While an advance of hushed
Words grow in you as a private isle or estate,
While you call those uncontrolled desires for thrill and travel
Our uncalculated, but mute search for a rather tall embrace.

Dietrich:

                        Yes, again, my love rises very
Cold with ambivalence, and I quit at nothing to void
The blanched feeling, which shall go on and on without
Firming a surge or a rich beginning or for
A rich ending. I am alone then within midnight without conflict. . .
                When this love, excellence of my touch, evokes no
Response, for the fear of place deserts a hovering dove. . .
When I try
Re-tried a wistful trace so hesitatingly, it'll come to disappear
There so quickly.

I sound like the lost they disown and report to
Despise. . .
                              But, here, I
Seek with you. . .you, relying on no more ground from
Distant harmony. We're, by comparison, strange and maybe, now, old;
We don't submit to the times nor pay the charge. . .
                        For us, I love you much
Longer than I want you to love bliss with less
Courage and trust. . .

Gertrude:

I wouldn't miss you so much in

This niche without the accents to a future. . .At this time,
We ask for things to be small like faint waves
In our blood at its valve. . .

But the opening task of

This peopled earth spurred by earthly nods and commissions will
Have something more obliging than the birth of a yawn
Or whispers. . .where life explores life without words, as near,
Mere events scale higher than the power of hanging metaphors.

You were too warm to deny. . .Much like a phrase
That doesn't disperse or music or uniform truth at large
With an inference and fancy for love, wearing many signs
That ask for receipt.

It was not by your dire patience

But by your energy that made me forget many of
The memoirs I'd formed of love. I would, with pure
Intent, have espoused so much desire if words had been
More successful, enthralling my reach beyond the aroused conflict of
Ideas. . .into an essential energy that begins and ends more
Entirely. . .

Whether I would love you held no plot, contained

In but words and subject to changes in your mystique.
No, the realm your body, by rushing herds, took me
Lifted the way of my trust – touching a lenient world
And molding an eager moment. It's the foray into you
I can absorb that remains as long, as full as
My own body can last, and no further. . .And veins
On which I dream also reflect the fears that you
Will be seized by the very supreme priests of gravity. . .

Dietrich, for God's sake, don't let death adjust

Or consume you, as though it were an impatient mother who
Expects you home at dark before you resume again. . .

Haven't

You breathed fear long enough to tell it was never
Intended to be satisfied? You throw the rough magic and
Looser community away whenever you have proudly chose a progress
Toward death. . .

                    The more you believe
Truth as a mere and abject corner, the further from
Reasons for loving anyone at all. Touch and tell to
Feel nothing I feel? Not unless you tell this democrat
Not to love you any longer. Touch and let us
Weaken if you wish to be saved above all else
By anything but our touch. Abstract pain puts us out of
Our nature, and we bless little and devour modest and
Plain portions.
              While I conclude to
Be more than I am, am I fit to be
Much less than I was? A woman, everything that can
Give birth, but alone, everything I access uniquely personal; and
Mostly unlike you, there are far fewer lessons I choose
With which to align myself. . .For my body will strike
Fire swiftly and then embrace victory and sport and completion
Yours can never hold nor intend.

Dietrich:

If I always defend myself, then I'll also have to
Apologize. But you, Love, can happily amend and gladly gather
Up those grand creative forces showing so obvious the
Nascent hunger that's still crying in you.

Gertrude:

              The rest of this world
Shall so much less easily regard others for the same
Style you invent for yourself – to clutch calmly that certain
Amount of death in a sweet composition you follow. . .

198

Naturally, I keep you like a sovereign and
Mature woman can keep you and, uncompelled, go keenly awake.

I could feel you balk, leaving with a faint notion
To contemplate the ethics of ancestral chalk, the residue and
Bone of ritual. . .If God were the god of the
Living, then how can we treasure solitude?
                              And yet, yet, you're so much
Safer alone, aren't you, Dietrich, on guard at all times,
With the pall of choosing between text and attachment, one
Over the other, and not choosing again at all, but
Wending away to divine at your own self-imposed pause and
Refuge? Nothing quite so compliant to confine in a world
With openness and elective being the bread to feed us. . .
To lose love by promising too little access from a hesitant
Display?. . .
                              Bland and noxious,
Waiting on a move, I'm piqued by your creations, Dietrich,
Your chide so well – I, partial heathen. . .
                              An extra limb,
Hand or degree you lacked before you could ever decide
You ever had a reason for my play. . .Along the
Way. . .No, I was given a glad life long before
I intimated bias or songs to enjoy it – we can
Not disguise a gift nor an undated grace that is
Wholly the act of richer love. . .Not a guise at
All! But while treating us as a testament or tact,
You soon imitate the search and eloquence of God to
Serve your own nameless and lonely lurch toward a message.

Dietrich:

                              Busily, we fear most alternatives most, for
They suggest danger there and a close to the recognizable
End. . .
                              For many ideas are hard as
The earth, and I get harder myself the more abstract

I wear them alone. I care for nothing, if there
Were no near marks for nearness. Bear with me, love's
No more an accident than grass is. . .While we treat
Hate to be foreign but love evermore present as another
Wish that's no longer in hiding.
                              So, if you ask
For my tenderness with obscure hints, the phrase falls to gibberish
Such that I can give no lines in return. . .With
No reply, love will seem just as easily a negative
Or damaged, or my love for you could just as
Easily be affection for myself. . .
                              Or can we consciously confuse
Love for another passing remark that transports us to a
Feeling that pleasures stasis but remains as dark as
A vague, but harmed season?
                        However, you now wait for full-blown
Proof I'll not deplete what I feel to which I
Do not attest. . .when the essence of discrete wording confirms
The sudden dawn of knowing. . .Separating myself from a common
Lot, disappearing from the icy breath, disabusing
The memory that haunts through verbal rabidity.

Gertrude:

I don't retain each of us in the world I report;
I withhold implications for each of us as I abstain
Even from the lightness that can ever touch us fast. . .
We grew here like two minimum fates, two platitudes, which
Rouse no milestone nor a resolution, blown out of the
Exercise of life to dry in some posture alone among
The dust of disinterest. . .Waving ghostly at our own revisions
With words to be heard quaintly by themselves and sparsely
Understood enough for the space of a lifeless profile.

                                                  Oh,
Dietrich, I still get angry whenever your fatherhood chooses to
Divide our fluent presence. . .We're vacant, a search without mission. . .

200

As though there's nothing yet but dissonant suspense left of
Fretful haste.
                              We're lonely without a home to put this
Love, love that needs the quickest and less frontier place,
For if it's not throughout a home, it ages and fractures
As its song can impel out the unhidden door.
                                              And love made too big
Made a difference – to be talked away among friends on
Nights that had our grief and slow time ruling near.
Someone, much like us, had degraded in the chief edge
And hands of government. . .The longer we sat and listened
To our voices and responded to the shames of the world that
Now survived through secrets about which we could refer but
Were afraid to inquire.

Dietrich:

What can be too true to be obscure? Recognize this
Face once more before it promptly tires of filling blind spots. . .
A face, much the part of a reprise. Will we
Have to wait very long for a pause to start
Honest looks again? Rely on some sure slang to shorten
The obscurity that takes us away by self-love from each
Other and lovers away from hot and abiding colors. If
I had one thought to invoke: Better lives shall convey
Us from these times, not for what the times do
To us, but what great crimes they make us commit
Against each other.

Gertrude:

Love nodding that you're too far away, Dietrich; the terrible gaps
Cut your contemplative interest until you can't tell above
Or below whether it draws along an elongated line. You
Doubtlessly do not want to hear or know slurs and
Ambiguities of my nature any closer – for affections lay weak

Against the cold, bare contact with the brave and unalloyed,
The deathly rings of detail. With my incautious glance at
Any static state, the more I choose to assail secrets. . .

Dietrich:

In gross ways, my own games end up teased by patriotic
Decay. . .And show traits of a lover prone to fail so many deftly
And mechanically. . .
                          Betrayal appears on more mouths, brothers anger
Brothers – even of the same blood, an impetus for murder rears
Less forbidden. . .
                          And nothing can protect us from the extremes that
Begin in fixture.

In early October, 1940, Hitler discusses with his new Polish Governor that workers required for German purposes should come from Poland, whose gentry and other leaders are to be terminated. Bonhoeffer has received notice that he is now prohibited from speaking in public. Toward the end of the year and through the early part of 1941, Bonhoeffer resides at the Ettal monastery in Bavaria, where he spends considerable time on his writing.

Act II
January, 1941
Location: Ettal Monastery
Near Oberammergau, Bavaria

Dietrich:

. . .For lies build a future that can fit them best
And forgive the murderer of acts in the field where
Murder will supply a complete answer. Sure, order leading terror
Wore out resistance, as one stare, alongside fraud and descent,
Raised the slope of evil in a country, stealing the citizen's
Own best place. . .And if that face should not cope
Or were defiled, the desires of millions would also falter.
Surprising most, the face, as all such faces do, beguiled
And would not substitute; and refusals of the face landed
Self-inflicted wounds, many found – they, with brute hunger abusing
The past, not a few countrymen then seen accusing their own
Of diverting a steady walk to new freedom. Should the
Face break down, the victories and profound talk cannot
Be repaired.
              Quick burn strikes against each of those who, engaging
The elemental and fragile force, had dared a concept of
The tame. How, in these unusual times, strength of the
Negative to express joy! . . .At that, those arrogant questions somehow
Give turns to the worst corner of our hopes: Who
Is valuable, who isn't? . . .Or who shall be ruined holding a better piece
For value, valued for silence and spread across both tolerance
And soft delivery?

How the birth of dismal descriptions next due
Takes the place of health. . .and greater tumult for
Peace, mislaid for the time being. . .

                    In a crusade of mighty dashes –
Another momentum to flow, as though God chose to test
Us through one more choice, which we, so amateur, must consider.

Richard N.:

    Once taken, the script this year no longer fails
To be lawful. And once taken, power shall no longer
Right itself – it is, and that's cleanly enough. . .It hunts
Through a rabid spell and has redoubled in abstract, much
Like murder defined as magic shall swell into repeated acts. . .

Voice of the Condemned, #097605:

Murder, an act of the cryptic, famous. . .When it's milder
To kill than to kill the larger reason for it – it
Came and it comes with less effort than a song to
Raise the rest of morning, wise and playfully done.

                    Murder, sharper than any doubt or
Confused passion, does not leave an abstruse line. . . Murder,
The avowed apostle of mute clarity and loud night. . .

Dietrich:

    A forced image behaving near in bald perversion,
A knotted creature to kill and ravage. Beware of dramatic words
And the damned prophet, a deadlier reach to
Every living thing. . .
                    When greed performs as a myth gone wilder,
When a trait does its business, a focus, also an alibi
Without fierce calm.

How much a late carcass can be
Smelled in the unreasonable garden, and we're left to manage
The swollen debris with the rest of the disease beheld.

Voice of the Condemned, #611019:

Then, history then joined to the mad crowd to be
Obscene, the old spirit explained away and coined as past.
The gently old parting first – they're the least, the least
Aware, the least in place, in the midst of thirst.

Richard N.:

A smaller scene appears to answer a person who has
Learned to live around lunacy, to snug to lost grace and
Forbidden progress when farce gathers most by the direct heat
Of disquiet. . .So many drawn to profess a bond with
The devil who sleeps through din and wakes for chaos.

Voice of the Condemned, #820211:

                          And still, as peace
Was inert and disguised as coy, they didn't even try to
Take it seriously but hastened away in bliss to convert
All trust and grace into weaker names.

What comes in mystery must, in turn, revise
Itself to stay tempting. . .

Dietrich:

Are we arranged in case the latest evilist tells
Us how to lie? Are we sensible enough to move safely out
Of the way? Does it not somehow matter why, curiously,

He's here or how truthfully he whispers that he can
Feel nothing but others infinity?
I watched him closely to see if he would talk
Back like an angry boy having bluffed and notched all
Those who unify after him. It's a story that goes
Without order, without one whisper or elemental sigh for hope.
Then, to play on several words for tests, we wait for
The next newspaper to stain the truth and hearsay we've
Been sure will be lost – in yet another flurry of
Bad opinions. . .

Richard N.:

                                    For, at these uncommon times,
We readily admit we barely understand the most absurd forms
Of everything we compare. Here, do we omit our praise
For the ways we like to heighten and hearten the altitude above
Shaded parts that hang mostly unfree in a pendant state?

Dietrich:

                                         But as for the
Maniac, a murder does not assure days of persistent ease,
For it is not murder that he wants, though murder,
Like theatre, brings an answer and an applause. . .Inside his
Own special pit and, thus, inside his own special fault,
Then, at last, he finally knows, after all the fuss,
That murder only looks like theatre.

                                      So many suggest we
Should play a maniac's game for a maniac's tale
Of belying, of molding parts that rage to the beat
Of kill. . .For in the heart of an enfolding and
Secret rage are unsatisfied, but extreme views.

206

Voice of the Condemned, #197713:

. . .As all this violence did not evolve from custom, but from
The frustrated worlds of an addled, bestial crave. . .Amid
Kills by circumstance, kills by season!

Richard N.:

                    The adage confronts
The practice, for how often you've said, "Whenever you're
Brought along to conform, the artifice alone can be glorified
And later into idols."

          Steadily, dogma shall kill just as noisily and as
Speedily as any hate or the slough of hell.

                  A consensus to prompt more than
We believe anyway. . .Is that the technique of self-love –
Elevating the way we will achieve more than our
Charity shall let us?

Dietrich:

Quickly, we say, the high theme of a search shall remain
An absolute now completely safe?. . .For, at the initial sign
Of power, desperate rule – the truth, when resolute, must be
Destroyed or, at least, heavily threatened to keep it shy
And limp. . .
             There, victims, none saved, reside distantly,
Debased in persecution and marshaled by an estate of so
Wrong a tilt – all of the taste
For history forgotten in a single, untaciturn moment. . .

                        Is there
Enough human concord and dissent allowed such that dreams and
Death are always jostling here, there for dominance and stuff
That legends, lyrics recite in telling an abundant story?

Voice of the Condemned, #083626:

Two fists begin to grab for the same and prime state,
And both come near with unique and dissimilar handfuls in
A rush. . .

Dietrich:

                    Oh, I jar at the cost of my
Fixed goal there to keep moments from becoming a foul and
Wild start, from becoming a cheap and lewd revel,
A local reply of desire seeking vile pleasure!

Do I merely ask that we not typify?

Voice of the Condemned, #841175:

Be right? While not with the right to outdo ourselves
Meaning rectitude, though rectitude has its bearings. . .A tinge of
Delusion, a tone for risk that charts the mood to
Delude ourselves, had better be left unsaid.

Richard N.:

It's all too close like someone who'll not leave you
Alone, who asks for those many grandiose schemes out of
Your claim. It's someone who does not favor you enough
And enjoys having tokens as a hard-won prize in
Hand to ease the zeal for more. . .
                                        Anything passing near as
A sign for a venue, altogether unrehearsed, will appeal, of course,
As little else can.
                            I plan
My world to have nothing but the entire range of

Achievable pursuits, like the entire world was created for my
Exhibition. . .and not my condition fashioned for the world's disputes.

Dietrich:

To watch, so it can stand, against which we judge all
Things. A couple of dull sounds; then, screams accuse;
Someone soft excuses, for the crude and loud, any rant
And acts to temper tragedians who do not hush nor
Pare the vows of incorrection or sin near the mass
Mind.

Richard N.:

How we check everyone
To think as we do. . .And how those we face
Want us seeing them the way they had seen themselves.
Don't import
Feelings for my sake – too many are doing that for
Us all already, forcing many into the mistake of letting
Their passions be much less by being less germane.

Dietrich:

That side for us does come
Private like a subtle answer, and that enduring trace of
Tender sounds simply had no other holy role than the
Role of its lightness. Yet, nothing shook then so much as
The response I felt rising in whole with my declaration. . .
As if desire and its target were inseparable parts of
The same impulse.

Hans von Dohnanyi, with Bonhoeffer's participation, organizes a program, known as "Operation 7," to use Jews in Abwehr, who are then able to escape Germany. The "Final Solution," as envisioned by the Nazis, means the elimination of all Jews in Europe; toward that end, extermination facilities are established by the German government at several camps with Auschwitz having the capacity to kill as many as 2,000 persons at one time in each of its largest gas chambers. On June 22, 1941, Hitler's army, along the Russian border, begins the German invasion of the Soviet Union, but, within only a few months, the Germans are stuck in the mud. Bonhoeffer and his co-conspirators decide they should accelerate their activities.

Act III
December, 1941
Location: Klein-Krossin Estate
Near Kieckow, Germany
Bonhoeffer convalesces from pneumonia.

Dietrich:

>   . . .And the walk
> Of a dawn reminds us the step altering clear grace
> Is very much alive.

Gertrude:

>   Calm had made them violent. . .No doubt, they'd treat
> A lover worse – the fun and crusade to garner by
> Transforming a lover into a stranger; and to do it
> So convincingly that they would never plan to see the
> Person they'd known ever again. . .
>   The eyes were so lucent
> I read they'd already forgotten and grown bored once more.

Dietrich:

> . . .If I had to admit

It all over again, I would not have tried to dwell alone
Nor to clarify so completely and awkwardly – it should have
Taken more enterprise, even more wry abandon.

Richard N.:

> I was cut

Roughly from the source and collection and stood up like
A part of damnation to witness the coarse and unholy
Soldiers take others with impunity, at the time thinking of
Everything I would do if they happened to lurch a
Move my way.

> Amid survival and guilt, there's a seizure

And no choice. . .Even then, how we try to prove
That we own something of ourselves. . .yet, plans for survival
Can't quite attempt to feature a half-grown cause. . .How I
Now reach to hide in cowardice that something I reluctantly
Call my own – the courage surely isn't there to breach
The context.

I'll be left waiting for something else to happen.

> I

Was alone without an episode or a right and deft
Voice; I wasn't famous or vile or even dismissive. I
Wasn't anymore caught with a choice than I am now,
With brief and broken interludes unfolding old personal answers to
Old personal questions.

Voice of the Condemned, #088825:

> In

Bigger moments, we'll often bear and abide like the youngest
And less fortunate child who must be cared for before
Any of the rest.

Richard N.:

If I said apostates looked binged
And too young for the grim things they were doing,
Would you believe I'd idly passed by and hung on
Such observations? When you're a victim, what else can you
Think of, other than the signs for a retouch of
Damage? There's no time to be wise nor to deny
Beautifully. There's not a spot and there's nothing new for
Which I'd sing even lowly. The door clanged like steel
Behind, and I stood there waiting for something fresh and
Plentiful to compose something soft and tolerant, maybe as a
Day or night that has no hours.

Dietrich:

There, I scoffed
No more at a fate – I could rest or bluff
Or behave, even scream, or bait without fear of reprisal;
For so long as I had wanted to be left
To myself. Yet, seconds passed headlong like stones resounding against
The chamber of my skull as something similar to immovable
Pains at being blanch and paralyzed did dull the proposition
That I was still alive until I realized that I
Was all alone. . .And none, by their own will, could
Now come back to confuse us with the innocence of
An old life that would wickedly use a body in
An innovative and able way. Desperation in a lonely room
Stirred like acid as it burned away in my blood,
And I could not think of myself any longer but
Lustily focus on fierce pain. It was not a link
To insanity, but to grief; I thought of silly things:
An iron wrinkle of a distant aunt's smile and disbelief,
And the twitch in my uncle's step, a place I
Had lost a long time ago, a niche that mattered
So little it was not even a memory, friends who

Were not friends at all but the unfit and bruised
Half of an incomplete thought. . .

            But I was not yet connected to prevailing times
Which had so much of a direction and no counterplot – I
No longer proceeded with anyone whom history could have judged
Still slightly relevant to the acceded, prevailing course.

                                    No, none
To interfere with content when a new front rearranged shape. . .
Nothing left but the abstract of mere drama to keep
Score. I could devise myself as both victim and executor
Without changing a hair on my wild skin. . .and to size
Lure, as if hope and its lapse always surface from the
Same mold, though machinery for one reads sure disintegration for
The other – pleasure always being pain in the other.

Gertrude:

                                    Any
Act at all will have prompted displays of another life,
Which, from the start, can control the world to become
More faceless. . .An innocent torn apart without a faint regard
For anything he thinks, much like being caught in the
First column of first murders. . .By shadowy winks, by guilt
Or by eloquence, whether by shift or by a shot
In a ravine, death is death – with no lasting evidence
Of any retrace of the cold cause or fraught demeanor. . .

You're so brave you don't have patience with the rest
Of us wandering. But you're a reminder that a grave
State left resembles an excuse. . .
And to please and to placate the fettered devices of
This survival, I've nothing to give a soul but the
Description of the time I have waited. . .

                                When I wait for extra
Time to animate another choice I've roused and a compulsion
Begins to steer and manifest speed.

Dietrich:

                              The ritual melts
Into an accusation! I can't help with any of your
Questions, since I'm noting those covenant words to be said,
As if I were not listening at all. . .For now,
I'll be remembered for yielding to a whiff of power
I didn't respect. . .though I'm more parts of a scheme
Than I am of myself. It's a matter of suspect
Words that I don't consent further.

Voice of the Condemned, #237981:

But you did know the difference, or it wouldn't have
Been so hard to accept. . .Nothing to rid or recover
You from the imbalance which the decision was – a political
Pose bore no attitude nor quick glance to safe shelter.

Gertrude:

                                Only
For those imagined things which, held by us, can't use
Any other description do we save the word, love. . .Now,
It's safeless and harder, and mostly steeper than with quaint
Times when we gave brittle, perfect little things the title
Of love. If there were much more to adore in
Us, to raise conduct that could be understood so fluidly. . .
                I had to turn to imperious anger to recognize
Our common and softer themes – it's my radical nature which
Cannot admit its radicalism as long as by comparison
I cannot yet justify my own in opponents' eyes. . .

Dietrich:

                                                            Bearing
Danger as I look to govern and set in detail
My own style and effect. . .Still, soldiers go ahead through
Another body with clear faces, juvenile and fresher purpose and
Attacks. . .Spectators for our own lives, we are quite finally
A type of anticipation and anticipate an hour of everything
We see more cleanly than evil talents can take us.

Gertrude:

I cannot produce desires so timely, therefore, with so
Much gross abandon as I did before I saw the
Extreme wreck. I can be sure of one thing at
The site – we made a decision to resist hoping, which
Was made as much for something or someone else all right
As it was for us.

Voice of the Condemned, #751069:

                                    Alone, you'd say that silence
Is everything we should want to convey, a procedure to
Noise. . .Phrase upon phrase they brought disgustingly, as they did
Not wish anyone to modify the praise for any artifice. . .
For now, we live in a time of image, now
Infantile. Is it ever believed false?

Richard N.:

                                            A vow, a famous
Contrast to occur such that I'm slave, liberator to those
Being lulled into one more vast celebration of myth, dependent
Upon the figure they want. . .

Now, I must be complex
To be real. . .
And to flaunt, to save myself and
You, Dietrich, from the brutal and blunt conceits that ask
For a dishonest reply. I watched your heroic sweat confront
Its mission much like your blood answers its supply, so
Rash and too hot to shun the chill and turn
Of conscience.
You didn't laugh enough to be taken seriously. . .
Can you find enough friends and friendship to know
Others will give you sympathy?. . .
The beginning of country if
We could be so discreet; can it be of radiance
Or be merely patriotic? Beliefs resemble lies as they are
Gamed by any smoother and politic leagues, and the more
Powerful the group, less true the loudest thing it says.

Gertrude:

How an image soars when we stoop to damage the
Truth. . .
The original time I heard, you talked, Dietrich, and measured
Like there were no questions or disputes – you were immersed
As people are when they wait for one power to
Take them to another life that's possible and irregular. I
Wanted more than your silence. . .
It's strange how
Acts will explain the reasons we stay quiet. Some abided
To hear a speech, and you, so urbane, were pursued,
For they would not belong without hearing your part. . .
When you observed rejection as
Another phase along freedom for your goals and even for
Those rejecting.
Was it a ringing quest of
My intent I'd rather declare than explore? Or in response
To others who think they can scare or coax a
Lie out of me to strengthen the reasons they want
Us to fail?

Dietrich:

A new world delves into a

Second chance at this life, another run at this one
Still with a pride of advance and reward. . .and a
Whisper to a fate that somehow power never works the
Same in us as it does forthwith in another.

Or,

Again, to plan to infuse our version of power to
Enable a better technique. . .

Yet, games and history refuse and

Repeat the tragedy of lesser days in order.

Voice of the Condemned, #410547:

There's this illusion to think that the drape of

A form shields us from the gathering heat, but it's
Just an old shirt of torn fields we continue to wear,
No matter where we happen to be. . .

Gertrude:

It's for

Love that we will suffer and cheat so much. . .even
To lie at subtle murder and to search for graphic
Display.

Then, with one stare, we wish to apply

No farther than the initial contact of an eye, maybe
Noting nothing at all, a formidable clan of numbness,
Growing quickly into a guided and the tempting side of
A lover. . .as though a shrewd disease that cannot rightly
Satisfy itself until it has secretively invaded another body.

Richard N.:

                And to listen casually as we will
Care if a phrase were said for a durable trace
Of constant affection. . .And to listen coolly as we will
Foretell neither to do nor to covenant a thing other
Than to listen.
             A choice cannot be borrowed any more
Than happiness can. . .though we listen for a voice so to
Lose our own as if it were never ours to
Have.

Gertrude:

         I've watched you wait, Dietrich, and muse about other times. . .
Your brooding times to change the times when change may
Magnify the worst parts of us. . .When we rearrange ourselves
And train again on an unsure march. Can you tell
Me if love will have a domain to hold? Doesn't
The strongest love withstand a twist of views without being
Lowered?. . .
                If you hush and
Say yes to progress, you must say no to love,
Which should consume deliciously. . .The first foments more flavorless and
Common score – deny one, the other defines you. . .Each one –
To be natively and selectively built before it can be
Ranked. . .

Dietrich:

                        What must
Start from no standard nor systematic run so that whatever
Happens is deftlessly natural? The valuable marks, this evidence
We recall. The world grows and begins from nothing, and
We come from nothing. Each step from oblivion tries an
Engagement and scheme of life, a minimum speech, then hastily

Going in a direction from absence. . .Or, as we demand
Cruel space, we drive all things and a related axiom back
To nothingness and primitive form.

Voice of the Condemned, #568791:

                   It's a matter that many had come
Around to hear you talk for no other absurd reason
Than they would believe in everything you might say. You
Had hope for awhile, as hope will always conceive of
Certainty by believing solely in itself.

Gertrude:

A self-vision locked inside a silent dream is altogether a
Desire for power. . .
                        Here, anything to ride quickly a mocking
Love through power will rate a generous haven of evil
Eloquence – always the source, cold clamor to many, the state
Is, by its nature, evil. Yet, we reach as though
Each time we hold the use of its lure, we'll
Turn it into a gentle phrase, much like those gifts
Of gentle lesson.

Dietrich:

                   It is more honest to learn to
Be clear than to hide an idea in a wasteland
Of gray. I catch myself here wishing to be profound,
But the few, decent ideas I have left lie garbled
Between a question and my last utterance simply at play.
If vague, I can't trust myself; I'm alone in my
Many words to be sustained or to deny the non-effect
They have. I yet will follow the chart of those
Words wherever they take me, for they are set as

Mine in a sea of currency and collection; but imprisoned
By my own obscurity and estimate, I resign myself to
Be both victim and the molder of an unshaped peace. . .

Richard N.:

For I wait on others to ferret spheres and stratagem
And a hint of totality, maybe a method to retrieve
Both a wealth of purpose and a tint that has
No glare but an object for which I am searching.
Of course, I discovered long ago we have, at most,
No technique nor blueprint – but seemingly, a mere wish; and
How droll the wish conveys in recognizable physique, how fully
We will ascend to someone.

Gertrude:

To sing, I'm part of you if ever you hear
My songs even in the inexorable heart of undoing whispers,
Those long a pitch in the direction of awkward darkness. . .
Or do you behold me in reflections of everything on which
We have disagreed?
                            You had taken the alternate from yourself;
You presumed to be freed by the thoughts and outlook
That were yours nearby.

Dietrich:

                    People and places affect us if
We will change, as all spaces and all the rest
Stand in imagined order that must be entirely new to
Be renamed. Able to believe in someone else, we command
A creating of someone new among the new to begin with
A smaller, an agile, and more halcyon world – such a
Better cast that finally stays still for a little longer. . .

And like that, we save all the warm and uncovered
Sides we care are true and truer. . .And let the
Heretics wander with conceit and suicides.

Richard N.:

                          The police did come;
We acted so that they had more rights over us
Than we had over ourselves.
                          No one stood; nothing was
Said. We looked at one another as though we wanted
Someone among us, who was misled, to betray each of
Us before we did it one to the other.

Gertrude:

                          The enemies. . .
                                    but I,
Nearly afraid I had dwelled and preyed on nebulous missions
More than I had conveyed or borne our motives. . .while I
Knew enemies never disappoint nor delayed any of our fears.

Dietrich:

The enemy and I, we constructed each other into apostasy
And did not fall for each other's story.
                                    None of us could
Any longer be well-guarded again; no, they looked at hands
To find soft spots and at our undiscarded clothes to
Confirm if we needed someone malevolent and well-arranged to be
Present. The enemy waited in a corner and conceded, saying
Nothing 'til silence strengthened their heedless stock. I would keep
Thinking how the silent event and obedience disclosed so much
More than we wanted to reveal, even more by gesture
Than anything any of us could have flaunted or confessed.

222

Voice of the Condemned, #721843:

A promised system, pray tell, shouldn't rise so cruel in
Its effect. . .The citizens awake to well-worn stealth and then
Defer in acquiescence, or they then exploit the weakness to
Be transformed in brief into a hidden power or vogue
Greatness.

Richard N.:

                              The police, in time, relied
On us to finish an imposed and elemental lie; if
We fought, we gave them the best excuse to consume
Us, but if we submitted and bought the reign, it
Spread an admission of guilt.

Dietrich:

                        We didn't have to interpret
The appearance: That was done to the hilt by their
Desire for sway. . .As characters in absurd plots, we'd neither
Fit into absolute zeal nor inspire ourselves to enter a
Threatening maze.
                           I watched the pleasure rise from subtle to
Heavy until they set us efficiently and notched us into
Their pattern; whether we had changed or lied held no
Relevance. . .Force seized them into one tragic and mad life,
Functioning incomplete in the range of a surge by delusion
And of regardless conduct. . .
                        And ridden by the elite to edges, we
Drop short with each leap we attempt, though each one
Must be tried so as to steep us in the famous
Words that we're at least partially free. . .

They told us we'd break apart in this world, for
We were ruined by all apparent and bold happenings and
Could not overcome ideas that were too fragile in a
Fight that does not wait either on some ethic that
Serves itself or on one of us moving toward a
Reason no one but ourselves, who're left behind, can understand.

On December 7, 1941, Hitler issues a "Night and Fog Decree"; anyone jeopardizing German security in occupied territories is to vanish without a trace into the night and fog of unknown areas of Germany; the order also forbids any such prisoner contact with family or loved ones, thereby allowing German authorities to abduct individuals who then effectively disappear. By the beginning of 1942, top Nazi officials hold a meeting in the Berlin suburb of Wannsee to discuss how the "Final Solution" can be achieved. Around the same time, there is an increase in the number of people and groups in Germany participating in clandestine opposition to Hitler and the Nazi government.

Act IV
April, 1942
Location: Marienburger, Allee 43
Berlin, Germany
Bonhoeffer, facing the audience,
     sits alone at his writing table.

Dietrich:

For no doubtful sounds now rest on fresh verbs
We measure and conjure during a tirade. . .

In the stretch of anger, wit cannot stay tall
As it but converts into weakness, a seed of grace
To be lost once a terrible might reverts ever forward
To a practical crux for the practice, which shall decree winning,
Poor winning. . .
Soon, revolution, new heaven, yes; it was so
Absolutely pure, like they could sue and heal a body
Of subterfuge with one, blunt vaccine.
        And unhurried,
There were those who thought another abysmal war had then
Stopped; like children, there were still others who'd doze and
Could not recognize the world in which they were abiding;
And as children, some chose to rise and dismiss it

And try to dictate, by conscious copy, a dread one
Existing falsely in a false phase or fantasy.
        Too many will ask themselves to be much
Better among their laws than they can ever construe for
Sure and fully explain; either there're too many laws, or
We give them too much fated strength. . .
                                I'm sadly convinced
That to fight terror, we can be lost in the laws
Of the aggressor. . .And
All the subtlety wore thin around the worn, and they
Responded to nothing unless it led to the obviously angry.
Unstopped, they could not let doubt stress a blank sheet
Against which to draw and set the best of themselves. . .
For a revolution, their pleasure, for which they groped and,
Perhaps, which was, even briefly, the value they understood to
Be themselves. The revolution to do evil and save illusion
That would be obvious to everyone and for the perpetrator. . .Splendid!
As we stare, as people were drained into surplus there
With streets to be dissolved by the elite traffic, we
Held to calling for more freedom toward the weak involved, who then
Could realize we had less. Have they been more successful
At anything than the overthrow of a sad, old system?
And if not, do they have anything more to be
Proud of than the degree of grand skill it took
To establish a new savage? So, they can rest new
Promise on a success to employ a devilish threat expertly
                . . .by undoing our possibility bit by bit

Until it disappears into the hunger that's teased and fed
By making it more unfed. . .
                As they confer violence onto
Every part, as violence so numbly institutes the deeply undiluted
Storm they possess. Like a drunk returns for another gulp,
They must return to the length of the source for
Clues. If they think an act stirs a dream to
Near completion, they look to ways that start to link
All to effect. . .
                   We now

Know it doesn't matter what others think if they stage
The suffering. . .Or if some trust us sacredly and we then commit
Murder, many may even think it's but our own loose form
Of justice. . .

        The Church puts its lyric on and
Hands in its pockets and pulls out the best it
Has and gives its agents frayed, slight threats to apply
And handle; the threads wear out. Soon, the next world
Lying evident as the heads of a calmer place
Will be less insistent, we suppose.
                          Within
Its composure, what does the Church choose? If its intent
Were union, it couldn't survive then solely being the Church.
If it chose to rarify and revive through the snare of
Prior charms, yes, it endures, but just so long as
We don't decide it fosters a relentless tale.
                               The
Institution deems to persist on the glory it has known;
While the Church lately redesigns regimes and twice merits of
Its prophets and a pact for the current lines of
Its retreat. . .
Yet, the Church cannot fail forever: It's a certain
Part of recall, and, like every portion there, it will
Rise to overwhelm the speed and start of decay. . .
Near the destiny of pure water in original rites.

What could I say to those who will yet listen?
That you came from the country, eager to be more
Than you even arrayed to be. Did you think a hushed
And naïve land was the familiar whim you were given
Without any history to contain it? On the eve of
Disintegration, which would quickly make young people of us all,
It also stood to make us clumsy among the more
Mature types. I wonder what would have happened if you
Had been born into some older years and old stereotypes,
Who fought alone to be believed, as they were stout as

Stones you would exorcise through revolution.

You shall now
Subscribe to a system that prepares more constant control of
One person over another, though it shall describe the opposite.
Isn't it fearfully possible then that at a different moment,
You would have denied this order for the same terrible
Reasons you now enforce it for all who come?

Or, like someone who knows how to talk
Too much, you talk yourself away from others. . .And how
Much have you added to the mawk, the volume? Is not
Much the stir around the reason you've committed with promise
To revolution hardly a defense for failure of the revolution
To reach its original sights?

That's the scourge of revolution:
You disclaim the past for which you lust to tell you
Who you are or to give you an honest claim
That instills all you finally come to collect and store. . .
After you kill the past, the slow, worst parts of
It can draw memory, hanging broadly over your last choice
Like the powerful wrappings of a shroud. . .

You can't
Treat the moment if you've already gathered the bodies. . .

What fills you when the times grow so ill, vacant
And deeply lost? You must defend yourself then from chills of
The onslaught of every blast. . .Do not casually turn your
Goal to the effects of a new course fraught with
Dreams you have hoped for, though they'll not come clean. . .

Compose the dreams, but do not treasure that
They'll either abate the pain we impose on ourselves
Or lift pain to a more ephemeral level. . .
Like choosing one chance over another, not because the size
Of conduct is inherently louder than the other, but because
It worked better than the other. To enter the region,
It's quite easy to be deaf and indefinite at the
Time you test yourself to fight for freedom and fracture. . .

Freedom unpossessed

Dropping like heavy thoughts that rest dull and neglected
On a molding monument. . .
                              Take private mercy,
Lost in today's politics and riding the rise
And fall of our emotions and not at any cost
To the power specialists at all, who shall hate. . .and we
Become freer? They nourish us with lists and routine of
Past mistakes we've made, and we grow stronger?
Is it strength? Do you though not know the calls
For which you are strong? A call can turn on you
Out of ignorance, just as you turn on it out
Of disregard. . .Oh, how failures teach circumstance and do not escape
Any or our way. . .

          And, like you, many of us have trouble
Giving wing to the dominance of the cliché of evil,
But merely because we have trouble with its heart in
The order of things doesn't, in the least, cause it
To disappear.

On April 26, 1942, the Reichstag enacts a law that gives Hitler complete power over the life and death of any German; the law also suspends any barriers to its implementation. The following month, Bonhoeffer meets with his friend, Anglican Bishop George Bell, in Stockholm to pass on a request to the British government not to attack Germany in case of a coup d'etat against Hitler. Shortly thereafter, Bell meets with a senior British official, Anthony Eden, to discuss the request and other information Bell received from Bonhoeffer on internal German matters, but Eden voices concern that Bonhoeffer may be used by the Nazis.

Act V
June, 1942
Location: Rathausgasse
Freiburg, Germany

Dietrich:

                                          Was it simply the
Allure of calm as the evilist did collect the smoothest steps
To withdraw himself either from exposure or from ceremony?. . .When
Antagonism filled his mouth greedily with special and raw themes at
The very time he was most convincing. I couldn't fight
Him face to face without a ready crime of forever
Thinking of him to be everything outside of myself. . .
                                         There, I
Would have as thoroughly fought a fine line that I
Knew unwise as I would have fought his becoming part
Of my voice. He stayed a damaged clue, caught in
My own defense – I wanted the thirst to be satisfied.
But separate from him, I constructed an unfettered sense and
Plan to take advantage of the others' wish to exclude
Themselves from civility, from things too real, from an adage
Too careless to believe. Surely, they would rather we hate
Them vividly than let them lose the hymns they'd not leave
Behind. And if they, for any reason, take us on,
We are sure not to mind their doing something half

Right, though, like us, they, at such times, hate themselves
More for languor than anybody has the ordinary and outright
Reason to hate the whole of their demeanor.

Voice of the Condemned, #814715:

I would have lied then
To save myself, not even splendidly, but by lore or
Something very meager or less; I realize daily, almost blindly,
That a gift from God is the eager cleverness to
Stay alive. . .
The changes, all changes, unwelcome changes escalate a little
Each time we shall arrive with a new hero. . .

Richard N.:

Do many conspire for the vaunted expressions in
The street when troops wait noisily in an attire of
Conviction for someone to meet them like most will for
A lover who's been away for love's sake?
The upbeat
Women wanting to welcome soldiers – and the children were owned
In the colors, and odd men were afraid of rumors
They'd one day join the ranks. . .While soldiers gathered a
Reason or two to be proud, for they had made a
Complete new world, and they could swiftly introduce most to
Its pleasures. They wished to blame us for our role
Degrading a report on the new practice, and collusive powers
Rose when lies began to name everyone by sport and
Failure. What a grand feature of the elite that in
Success, there are no real enemies left; but in failure,
Everyone near will have ravaged against the loss that was
So apparent. . .although one man, even with a cheer, can't
Lift the contents unless it's someone like you, who has the
Will to break a form and let the dense energy
Run out like fire over a frayed and colorless cloth.

The size of victory, so great a strain –
We mockingly in a sane world are found ever more
Often in a brutal one. . . A purity of pain
To try to direct us beyond the constant noise into
A compound of finer dialogue. . .where useful people wait, waiting
For the thinned direction of a better motive to soften
The effects of this hard and afraid country. . .

Voice of the Condemned, #579009:

A soldier means little but for the legions of approval standing
Behind him. He can create no elegant scenes nor a
Sequence further than the world he protects. Yet, at times
When blood roars, justice declines into a curled and unemployed
Phrase. . .

Richard N.:

I was born three miles north of Freutenstad in the
Shadows of wise, dark trees – my styles have been somewhat
Cold ever since. I presumed much faster than others did
As counting came so quickly; they have told a story
That I built two lightning rods with my baby spoons
Well before I was three.
                                    Even now, the quilt of
The land is quite mysterious, so I try nothing until
I see a final run in some finally tight and
Bare signs.
                                    And my father,
Comfortable – he had dreamed of that which agrees with vain
Politics. My mother too was sure also of her place
But had no creed for more genus. . .as a fix
Over the town spoke a pace of decline the way,
With too much declamation, one ruins a son, lying down
On an inviting earth with too much delay in the
Warmth and rain.

But the revolution at first was worth
Little there, for it changed mere margins there. Oddly, one's led
To be free to alter the estranging habit. . .and when
Speeches were given in the cities, the stores in our
Town were to be brushed clean. . .And the government preaches long
And promptly passes into apartheid in haste; we saw then
An old woman seeking another plate and more weight.

Dietrich:

To conclude that no force exists without help, even passively,
From the people it governs, and, as such, the flow
Of government collects the costs of our human failures in
Laws to protect us one from the other. Here, it selects
Threatening parts and touts enough lies to let us
Be innocent of sin. . .
                                  Everyone wants
To be moral; even the murderer feels best if he
Knows he's killed a favored prey to gather laurels he
Sought to land.

Voice of the Condemned, #447126:

                  . . .If order can control by word, then timely
Words had made the difference thus far. . .

Richard N.:

                                    Old men in
Their way will have touched the hard fortune heavily used
To convince them it was right to sacrifice the many
Innocents implicit in the mercury of violence. . .
                            Old men in town talked
About things to say as they couldn't have sung smugly
About their future. We knew the time string made no

Sense without them, without every siren or lure each old
Soul could reduce to a watchful chant. The old men
Did not wish to limit nor loose oldness, which shared
Wistfully in much union and contrast. . .They surely learned if
They were brave, they did not clutch at things that
Were violent. . .And if old men were violent, they were
Not free.

          They are called to prefer faithful knowing over
Imaginary deeds: Old men needing less freedom than they often
Have if they're going to be freer than they are. . .
To wider slavery was the intrusion of more rhetoric. . .They
Must survive for those who have been younger than any
Of the rest and now begin entirely new ways! For
I was young, so a new world could vow a
New credo and was made believable; soon, I must have
Found the events leading the revolution were done so
With our fears, not daring, in mind.

                 And an old
Man, reflecting the one town, reflecting also the exaggerated myth
Of an old nature, stopped short to shout at my
Slant, 'Have you considered any other dropped dogs? Don't beat
Them worse than they already are. You need them to
Remind others that you have an obvious plan for power.
And me? Do I comprehend somehow then exactly? Does my
Antique body tell you or once intend exactly everything that
I have learned or chose to learn? Have you thought
You're too close to a final phase to be concerned
About a phase for an exit?. . .As my hands don't
Work anymore because they're now too stout and weigh too
Much – is it within the failing that our frailty is
Again going to lead us?'

              And he'll sit and direct
While he says, 'Small things are for mercy, don't you
Know that, yet? We need less than a great call,
A great torch, or an unlimited freedom – these too quickly
Tempt to love all comers all the more.

              How we

Decrease yesterday's meager gains as an oppression by habit. . .And
How or why do we embed the peace and goodness
And convenience of growing old like an old pine tree?
These can guide with past spells, by reference to
The coming of earth, when by thirst for a return
To pure lucidity, a long homecoming and birth will have
Come around once again.
                        You want me to be pleased?
I'm now given over to newfound ambition so that I
Will not have to rest when my old age can
Have very little to say. So, you're going to test
And interpret my value – now, this time, you'll take the
Least grand method of contact? That's yet not to ask
Me a thing. Just assume this old dog wants to be
Described by the town with zing in a giant room
Where he has lived.'
                        The old man wiped his forehead
With the palms of blanch hands and relived there seasons
Left behind; using a bass mutter for length or tour,
He raised both arms and then, as though oddly deft,
Backed warily, tracking the several words to keep the recall
And warning intact, 'And having lacked calm, you still can
Not change everything I've done in my life – already, my
Past shall turn on you as one creation you can
Not explain.'
                        Was he so old that no scheme encircled
The monologues, attending to a report without gain or
Cause? I hear the words, as they go down into
The earliest mystery I have of conduct and other laws.
                                                During
Those times, we heard a lot we'd like to forget.

It was a flagrant burning away of blurred things that
Were left too long in the family attic, and the
Shedding would take place before any more mean work shall
Begin. After a few more months, I never heard the
Praise of the past undermine the new logic in any
Phase of the newest paradigm.

236

To think of it, I
Believe he must have wandered off to another remote town. . .
That was before I went to the capital city. . .Not
Many are pleased in uncertain times – not those with discontent
By loss or who lose themselves left in the wreckage. . .

Dietrich:

Of course, a revolution must dispel the setting and pages
Of the struggle and rearrange the chairs. . .but retrieve there
Those times that breed and establish destruction in the cold. . .
And undo the best of us, who hazard several phrases toward
The future. . .for it's not in a game that we
Succeed.

Act VI
June, 1942
Location: Kalckreuth Home
Munich, Germany

Richard N.:

                                        Have
We ever loved something so that even our tender stakes
And whispers do not do it justice? We recognize the
Love if we have known it as it extrudes gladly
In solemn privacy. If we have, then we see
Even this firm nature can be a passing fifth column.

From days of general terror standing in an age
Of delusion. . .But I've still never loved in narrow ways I could
Have loved, and now among the suffering the hordes can
Inflict, I'm not kept near where I would be, far-flung.

Voice of the Condemned, #317791:

If I were less free beyond the call, no doubt
I would be one of them. . .Do I confess to
Believe in freedom, or do I think it is but
Distaste for this natural world? Then, there are yet some
Who crudely accept this life as stolid: A moment that
Is made special only by the frailty of a comment
Or a nerve disorder gone awry!

Dietrich:

                         No warm days left –
They seem to pass us by – hot days to serve
To get the sting of winter and disappointments out of
Our deep muscles. It's basic to be set wrong here,
Left behind on a short excursion, delivered to no place

In particular. . .when I know I'll miss the heart of
The matter, when I cannot tie the essence to
Violent ventures over a cold land.

For awhile, every plan or
Page almost disappeared, like someone had stolen my rush of
Rages and paled them such that I couldn't boast of either
A greed of isolation or a greed of comfort, the
Need to be with none and the need to talk.
In the glare of collective madness, I was not the person
I continued to expect, though the stare of those who
Did not know assumed I had become the last, best chance
That remained after our safety was looted and consumed away. . .

Oh, there's no one I believe I can change, or,
Even falsely famous, save by a line that fares well,
As I can remember to say by rote or by
Sympathy.

Voice of the Condemned, #112028:

Things must be
More than habitual or correct in the recent morning – they
Must raise a cause for a form of justice, as
The truest things don't leave us in a pause or
A panic.

These times, talks of survival, are a style
Of lying to each other. . .
but surviving spoke back to let us
Know we'll wake mornings marvelously dying, always vast and raw.

Richard N.:

It's the habit of things I miss most now
When I am at this fragile moment that fits the

240

Mood of the current world. Who will wend into the
Lanes of an unsafe episode? History was already clued in –
How crimes worked within the damage fully molded by
Those past events – the cold estate that lurked barely beneath
Knowledge had ratified most of our misgivings. Now, we are
The results being pursued and rarified in the soldier's task
He likes to inflate as full compensation for danger.

      The soldiers – they must repel those who dare
To keep them from crimes they'd like to see, the
Times they'd like to deliver and the heroes they'd leap
To be.

Dietrich:

                How easy it is
For you to think in a gentle word of yourself,
Of me, of us – in any condition other than this? It
Yet seems harshly too serious that serious roles are
Too perfect for any of us. I do retrace how
Then in seminary – the world never did reflect my cut
Of it; the world leaned always askew; but now it
Lies ever more aligned. I gleaned too well the reason
I'm here delayed or the reason they strain to
Imprison me in myself: They fear to find when soon
Illumed, I'll not stop.
                Is my choice then loosely designed,
Looking like one more hour of fantasy, holding, at least,
A nearer part of history to mirror or infer the
Closest yearnings?. . .

              Can we be realized or merely poised in
Token events to prevail? The truth gets so worn out
While it's hidden in the struggle – yet, we don't fail
To live for more, as we cannot forget discrete features
Of its corpus. . .We daily chant all it will give
To us or the fast talk we've wanted to carry

This far.

       Still, it takes a mark absurd reminding us of truth
Again: An empty church or prisons replete with confused rakes
And victims, souls who serve slightly a piece while the
Dead had wanted a better country to deserve. . .Following rumors
That wade through the streets, trailing to spot the guilty
To prove the rumors were true and should not fade –
Most diverging knew the dying was once again another mere
Tactic to rid the world of the boast of innocence. . .

Richard N.:

                                     I
Would often worry about myself in relation to others at hand –
If traits could be honestly waived in any select moment,
If a site or a casual method, if abundantly wished,
Could ever make a difference – or through many trades, we
Must be played by a sense of the
Rise and fall of political pose. . .

                      Here, I judge myself
By the swerve I have toward the small recourse to
Myself. . .
       I affect myself in many
More ways than I can control or cure. . .
                         With passage in mind, my
Afterthoughts of someone else noting my traits start a summation.

Voice of the Condemned, #910116:

                         . . .We can't, somehow, in our
Shyness to be contained, consider ourselves either useful or suited
For the quick and altogether sustained in this wrong age. . .

              If killing for the sake of molding laws to
Balance both war and love of something, they must craft something else
To live. Or if they destroy the chance to seek, they

Create something to replace the search. Not a whiff can
Be taken away. . .

Dietrich:

If we were just so obvious as the scene that
Is so wrong. . .But we try to blur or color
Stints so as to cut them short to be manageable. . .
        While the comity gets
Harder and harder for each one of us to believe
The other, it means that all this grand doubt does
Happen in a spell that was foretold as a standard
To occur here. . .The walls and well feel a bit
Colder, and the mats crack a lot more. . .

I don't need objects or evidence the way I did;
I don't fight the way I did.
      In all respects,
I'm getting weary of all that promises more than I
Have yet received.

Voice of the Condemned, #506790:

      So much silence so valuable, overt
. . .To spread ourselves here and exist without good passion on
A whitely arid and meager plain?. . .As the more we read
The need, the louder it became, as our constant gaze
Wore out the survival often seen in revolt, so that
The hunger remained, for that's all that was expected. . .
            The
Body cannot fill itself, but it deigns to keep
On eating until the hunger to survive will have eaten itself
And its vanity.

243

Dietrich:

       The enduring harm, the grinding ache, pain –
I take these as methods, almost a discipline, an alarm
To focus myself into acts and apt language.
                                To suffer,
That is to be free, a draw on copious cataracts
To defy the apostasy from peace and mercy. . .markedly here,
The heretic shall magnify the warp of raised mediocrity. . .

                                         And
The lies and the dismay devising a better chance for
Mischief than I can estimate or could have dreamed anyway.

Gertrude:

. . .And the contents will run like light water into
The oceans that swallow and fulfill a refuge of change –
Moments don't even last long enough for a thought to
Be explained – can we understand an unfast choice?
                         To the dangerous, we're not yet danger,
And we can still be used, though there's no kindness
Nor agreement.

Have you read anything catching so briefly the message of
This brave letter we received from my sister? Part of
It I'd like to share with you, for the undeceived
Attitude of a day doesn't last too long. . .This country,
Something foreign and so much more remarkably lewd, Dietrich, when
We've had enough of many bad players who quell.
                                'You
Are missed, Dietrich, more than any others would be missed,
For you knew us so well, while we'd persist in
Tales and needed someone to stitch up the family's refrain
Often; wars disperse families the way, the same conceded way,
That a landscape is disfigured by random seizure. Dietrich, you'll
Behold everything I mean by this – we don't escape by
Talking about the future at home anymore. The songs keep
Us from thinking about the present rout, and we desire

244

A lull from the next vicious report. There's no one
To rely on anymore for shaking excess, for God's sake,
From the newspaper, when those yielding minds can be blamed
For the cheap manner that the news is read. Mother sought,
Faced with struggling limbs and braced for the next fault,
Angles for a clear sight of you, Dietrich – we chased
Our exchanges for possible signs of you. Most tend to
Agree with my verse, as I've recently inherited the sour
And rude role of obstructionist since you left.

Today, I

See the single and suspiciously whole freedom you had and
The power you exerted over us all. Yet, one thing,
Dietrich – we don't doubt the deserted ones as much as
We had to receive the harsh side of your intuitive
Voice for doing so. There's nothing seductive nor softly obeyed
Enough happening to any of us to urge us down,
As we linger about the cruel deviling that won't go
Away and has spelled the dark history to renounce. Someday,
We'll talk about better parts of our hectic and compelled
Country, and we won't disturb dogs at the site where
We've tried to delay them – our constant wish to curb
Their scoffing howls.' She ends the letter by telling of
The onslaughts so many compare, the routine that contends we
Should always inspect a better side. Friends talk much less
Now than they ever did when, in any respect, there
Were so many more of them with whom to talk.
Subjects are different now, and everyone can ignore each other
Somewhat better, for they are much more frightened of each
Other than they've ever been, especially waiting for the cruelest day.

Voice of the Condemned, #735956:

We'll too be bound to this greater dystopia,

Though there's little doubt we didn't dive into the feast
So well; it's not that we're part of them, but,
Rather, we were too close when the plunge and deep swell
Began.

Dietrich:

For as truth turns less important than survival. . .For as
Bitter as I resound, survival, to most, stays colorless and
Native truth, loosely confusing right and wrong. . .Can we forecast
Leaving one or two to negate the many who live
Simply by then counting. . .?

They come again, the night panthers after my curled and
Covered soul, who take equal pleasure in having my body
First.

Act VII
June, 1942
Location: Klein-Krossin Estate
Near Kieckow, Germany

Dietrich:

                I have come
To see nothing to show that history happens to assert
Itself as a linear pace to better times. Actually, the fate
Of us taken as a pleasant progress for each mile
Can merely indulge the next mistaken twists of a mind.
                In this nation, a hard rule has
Ways of tripping into codes and reverent names, as if,
By nature, events do happen that come to be best
For mostly all, so they say. . .Doubting this rhyme, I
Watch then for any vitreous signs that decent views
Will not be translated into an act or specimen of
The truth, that power plays itself out daily above the
Exercise of truth. Many, even uncouth ones, didn't say
So, but they learned power had rendered truth useless again –
At least, moral truth useless, as an unrequited cliché rose
Too large for any to resist, and soon truth had
Nothing to do whatsoever with work to imbue the last innocents.

Richard N.:

How we adhere to names like fine moths to a
Dim lamp; I suppose that as power joins to the
Squares of a choice, we find that damp and mildewed
Names are often the solitary sign we will have to
Express in a lasting and safe realm. . .
                Following a star or
Choice already socialized, we think a higher brand of freedom
Directs our next option and route; yet, we've but then realized
A part of a coalesced and tangled past.

Voice of the Condemned, #917643:

        To be so honest there means not to
Be there at all. . .So, the honesty is cut off
Before it can be named. . .honesty, in peril and penalty,
To be null over protracted time before we shall begin
Again. It's as though the deniers know the place we
Want to go, but the place of refuge quits and
Dissolves before we ever reach it.
                        With one way to impede them, we'll make
Ourselves over, catching them short before they change the game,
Whenever they'll contrive new rules and resort to new claims
For games yet to be played. . .

Gertrude:

It very well may be this time has also been
Constructed for us all to confuse the style and display
Of rules. . .For as we lurch toward chaos right away,
We've chosen something dangerous and large, of an irregular degree,
To make us part criminal. But if we measure the
Sense and health of the country's magnitude and promise, we start
With ourselves gently, closely, surely. . .

Voice of the Condemned, #716913:

                        You,
Like so few, have lots of dreams if you think
Times can now change. . .As some will strike the new
Tone and surprise themselves by concluding that there is one
Last ethic to be tried and known, put in the
Basket of wares we carry and call, for no better
Word, history.
               You, like so few, amuse us with airs,
For you think the rest of this world will think
As you do. . .What if something as another best miracle

Happens and you constrain the devil, how would you be
Sure in your search to expunge and restrain all you
Judge as wrong and unearth a fair garden for us
To manage and to harvest long after the devil has passed?

Voice of the Condemned, #034789:

We're tired of listening for an ethic; if we
Weren't, you'd be received, and the tyrant wouldn't have acquired
The country as a personal yard for those arrogant romps.
Your ethics attack with little force or guard, especially as
The walls they had become are weaker for reasons that
Have everything to do with the collapse down many halls.

Dietrich:

Oh, winning results in high ways to be moral, although, here,
The technique forms distant from any conscious role of the
Ethic. . .
      As a matter of style, the method evolves out
Of a paradigm that is both practical and politic, for
It is just on this most dangerous ground that wars
Are won or lost.
                The method to fit, the tack
For winning, must contrast with the moral – we have quickly
Found so many, in the gust of these years, saying
That to fade sends the highest mode of conduct. . .Yet,
We've heard the most useful is one that tends to
The tools and the gears in this upheaved land, which
Puts poets and theologians to the ground and foremost fears. . .
                                   We're
Enemies of the state because we think aside, but then
We're shortly enemies of the laws to think at all.

Surely, the gear in method can't assure the method is
Humane or sane, and those who conjure and steer plots

And craft well cannot be the best then to
Take a country. . .Someone's slight wordicraft at persuasion should have
Nothing to do with either the right or the knack
To decide which of us should or will live too
Or drown.
While a salesman can beat us, we don't
Have to use the stuff he's selling, but plan on
It, we're stuck with the politician we instate.

Gertrude:

Of the allure of events pitched too close
To the danger warned, do you hear someone there rattling
The gates after he, under spell, has heard the gatherer?

Richard N.:

We aren't here simply because we're closely tied to the
Dead faces or to the time and shrine of a cause
Or scrim we know to change because it needs a
Change. No, we study symptoms for change as though fate
Makes all things doubtful. . .for fate itself is famous with the
Headlines of today read final or strictly fixed, though they
Are flitting. . .
But to be current is ever bit so
Slight, so laced and badly hampered that we have meant
To bury the surprise of vogue headlines by a swift
Recapture of the more traditional face and former size.

Gertrude:

We sealed our turn a long
Time ago, and we have been modulating through a narrow
Choice for sometime, or so it seems. And lately, we've
No questions left – they're all waiting unfilled in our faint voice

250

Or evaded vision. . .

                     And we don't attend to results nearby
Anymore – they're a rough chance to have us argue rightness
Again to assure ourselves it was for good cause we still
Stood firm. . .

Voice of the Condemned, #420829:

And, yes, encumbered way, yes – recall the times we were
Too silent to hear the just scheme from those keenly
Longing, who could no longer listen but, learning to talk,
Gave themselves a job in the fight.
                                  That's not
The way it is around the innocuous many – brittle, disappointed
Folk who will keep repeating a tiresome day for cadence,
When time apparently never moves and deep power seems no
More brutal in one year than another. . .

Richard N.:

                                So that, more
And more, we are as free as the heart of
The place lets us be free, but, more and more,
At the time, a hard edge sets us closer to
The very reasons we are secretly free.

By the fall of 1942, Germany has acquired an extraordinary amount of territory – from the Atlantic Ocean to parts of Russia and from Norway to northern Africa. However, Germany's fortunes decline rather rapidly; by late 1942, the Allies make substantial advances in northern Africa, and the Russians control the Germans at Stalingrad. In October, 1942, Bonhoeffer and Dohnanyi hear they are named in an investigation that involves money transactions related to "Operation 7" and certain anti-government activities at Abwehr. In early 1943, the conspirators think the overthrow can begin with a bomb placed on Hitler's plane leaving Smolensk in mid-March; however, the bomb does not explode. Another attempt at the assassination of Hitler also fails. On April 5, 1943, Dietrich Bonhoeffer, Hans von Dohnanyi and his wife, Christine, Dietrich's sister, are arrested. Christine is released a few weeks later, but Bonhoeffer and Dohnanyi remain incarcerated for the rest of their lives; charges against them by the Nazi government expand during their imprisonment.

Act VIII
April 5, 1943; The Day of Arrest
Location: Marienburger, Allee 43
Berlin, Germany

Dietrich:

I think about solitude
More than I used to do – a mere premonition before
I draw a harsh future? For I find I want
To be alone more than I ever have, earnestly at
All, though I've never been alone so much before in
My life. Yet, when away, I think about home even more,
As though an evil pall exists by some final and
Grave sentence there.
Yes, I miss the many I love –
Of course, friends, more now – they cannot travel to
The next frame – something to do with how steps fall. I
Don't try talking quite as much, out of context, as I
Did, for I have more to discern than I

Have to say.

        Friends, who had never refused me, reply
More slowly when I need them in a hurry. I
Don't rely on jokes anymore to get me by gloom
Or tricks at stolen scenes. I grew much older than
I thought I would in a short time. Among romantics,
I am pale to give advice. And I don't seek
New settings anymore either, for the pattern does fail to
Give its pleasure anymore.
Oddly, the ones dying ahead had the most surprising days
Alive; if at all wise, I know survival and tons
Of evidence are mostly dry education. If we wish to
Endure coolly for no particular notion or sense, then there's
No particular gain to the time we've extorted, even from
The appearance of things. . .We learn, not by regular practice,
But by belief in something solving a still durable mystery. . .

        How, somehow, it's exceptionally invasive and
More grievous to consume our value with longevity. . .

        A moment insists, meant to be astute
Now as if I were to instill and envelope myself
With every thinker that has brushed the same vow and
Rock I have. And I daydream a lot instead and
Listen to others and remember things, a stock of flight,
Mostly forgotten as I decide where to stand. Or I
Foretell reports to come that free me from the natural
And constant thought about those I'll remember but will probably
Never encounter again.

Richard N.:

. . .Such a war, a catastrophe, raised by an unclean,
Human apparatus, collects acute loss in rapid instants. . .And the
Catastrophe is kept large by calling it a necessary root
Or toll of history. . .

        New machines, times force
New allegiances, wresting others into other enclaves. . .

254

                                       The course acquires
Its way doubtlessly – it's clear of bit players, other contrivances
And all that reminds all of mere fashion. And the faster
That's done, more reliable lies the course over the land,
Building a new order in a little less time. . .

Voice of the Condemned, #011725:

                           The rightness we hype when it seems
So obvious, though the display of the angle could rightly
As well have been directed in still another way and
Could have also been wrong: War gives too many perfected
Rules to those looking casually at conduct; for it is
Expected after the famed battles for the victors to bring
A thick moral to the reason the other side
Finally lanquished. . .As the moral can justify any sick purpose
For any war and divert words from an honest search
Toward those who would mark, mine and insert the blood.
With the weakest bearing blame for the dead, a comfortable
Violence comes as an option. . .The world connects the shame.

Richard N.:

The soldiers care for each other – do you notice the paradox?
I soon found the absence of any breach among them,
Equally obverse to the way they treat victims. . .They've launched
Into more bizarre feats and placed another extreme curse onto
The weakest, but whether by subterfuge or scheme, they then confide
In each other delicately. . .

Voice of the Condemned, #626380:

                        It's not that we misplay the soldiers
When they race so high, swarming, a faceless horde of
Wasps – they're too sure the base world they build won't

Be complete until all of us are wrenched from everything
We thought we were.

Gertrude:

                                        I'm not often conclusive any of
Us will ever then trust in the adage that we
Can live inside the truth. For when prompt and enduring
Absolutes are further from the sounds or the stride of
Power, there's a long use in sacrificing the known. Yet, for
A test, the draw of who is right or wrong,
Of tenderness and avarice, shall still be sports people play.
                                                        Our
Heroes are constantly ablaze by passing through an abyss – a
Will to history. . .to disavow work of a pitiless leader. . .
While another does nothing to stop, to still the offence.

Voice of the Condemned, #197865:

The malicious maneuvers to exclude include greatness of a kind:
A glaring light beyond all simple light, a barbarous pride,
No preserved candor, instability by the strict consolidation of thought
. . .A vague, but old and reserved allusion that has gained
The trance of familiarity. . . as a sound wears out its
Words. . .as the drone kills everything that purports a radiance. . .
And the rest who listened too little hear less and
Have confirmed it would be best to be entirely deaf.

Voice of the Condemned, #745014:

                                                Pose,
Source of proof, dares a citizen into submission, trains another
To invoke heavy movements, to control snares of pain, to export
Starts of danger. Hypnotic chants: The nature they effect to
Inflate the flaws and the storied parts of us and

Objectify them into a monument to be jeered and codifed;
The flaws, all the time buried deep, a testament in
Us, our secret weapon. . .
                              Hence, we hear songs of unviolated
Blood rather than mixed answers, rough recall, regret with courage.
Do we accept the serial type, the more managed form?
A more efficient world can mean a more impractical one.

Dietrich:

I am never without reasons; they come to me too
Dark to disguise, young and also stout, light as unmeasured
Light. In a versatile and strange way, they resemble liberty
Without delay. . .
                              While I explain as though a still better
Reason is always the best outcome of engagement. . .But reasons
Can also bring chaos, for they'll never be at rest
Until we dilute or diffuse the least they've ever said. . .Past
Voices have also learned.
                              Nothing's told so fairly to use
Us truthfully and thoroughly, and the past isn't quite ready
Nor as forceful as the public news already at hand.

If I can believe in more than something reasonable, I'd
Like to sustain and quickly retrieve it. . .as reason still
Continued a desire, even as desire was barely restrained by
Reason.
                    I infer scores of many imbued with doubt selling
A return to a time so fixed. . .But that's all
Meaningless to those who can foresee a stern future so
Greedily they establish no restrictions on it. . .
In a time of extreme answers, extreme questions are hardly safe.

Gertrude:

How I conform to new adventures more rapidly than I
Distinguish them at all; general delusions of reform, sketched often,
Are so much easier to hold than the lowness of
Singularity – a personal act, a peculiar notion needed for show.
                                                                      The
Already announced results, tribute to the marauders, catch most short –
With success trying to convince us of surety through insults.
Yes, I'm deceived cheaply on behalf of a future I
Had never seen but couldn't neglect.
                                        Consider the perceived progress –
It charges that we exploit all matter and temper to
Conduct an unambiguous end, but we have no more adroit
Calculus than our common and confused noise. . .
                                                New shapes teach
New size – we're called to the last, perfect tower.

Voice of the Condemned, #348127:

                                                Within view of
The actual, we're publicly more afraid with each thunder of
Loose bombs, combing and darting so near the zone
Of panic – they'll stop someday, but when we're brokenly removed
From the trap. . .
                    Though we fought
Closer there for every life than these remitted winners, who
Hunt us, these neighbors favored by air without selves to
Explain.

Dietrich:

They step loudly, steps ricocheting against the center, vital part
Of an inviting, this inviting heart – pulse momentarily convinced! I
Feel no drift waiting to be struck by loud resolve
Once again. Do not stop them. The swift fever must

Have a chance to expire, as consumptive fire purges
Altogether.
       I sense the heat of torment advance close now;
Let it follow one intended course. At last, let my
Pain wash entirely in weakness.
                        I hear martial, extended
Sounds. Unlock the doors. Free the house, this den of
Cold resistance. Freedom comes. Don't wait for one more knock.
Open the house, open the doors! Do you love me?
Then, don't deny them this slaughterhouse. So, do you love
Me? Then, lead them by access. Do you love me?
Do not refuse them. Do you love me? Feed them.

Postscript

Two years following their arrests, Dietrich Bonhoeffer and Hans von Dohnanyi are executed at separate locations (Dietrich on April 9, 1945; Hans on April 8th or 9th, 1945). Two weeks later, Bonhoeffer's brother, Klaus Bonhoeffer, and another brother-in-law, Rudiger Schleicher, are also executed for their roles in the conspiracy and the assassination attempts against the Nazi leader. On April 30, 1945, Adolph Hitler commits suicide.

About the Author

J. Chester Johnson is a poet, essayist, and translator. His writings have been published domestically and abroad and translated into several languages. Johnson, whose work has been praised by leading writers and critics over a few decades, has authored numerous volumes of poetry, including *St. Paul's Chapel & Selected Shorter Poems*, second edition (St. Johann Press); the collection's signature poem remains the memento card for the thousands of weekly visitors to the Chapel that survived the 9/11 terrorists' attacks at Ground Zero. As *The New York Times* noted, "'St. Paul's Chapel' has been used for the church's memento card for more than 10 years." Johnson and W. H. Auden served as the two poets on the drafting committee for the retranslation of the Psalms, which is the version contained in the current edition of *The Book of Common Prayer* of The Episcopal Church; the retranslation has been adopted by Lutherans in Canada and the United States and by the Anglican Church of Canada; it was also adopted as the preferred (now, permitted) Psalm version until the Church of England produced its own in 2000. Johnson's memoir and literary and historical commentary on the retranslation of the Psalms, *Auden, The Psalms And Me*, is forthcoming. Johnson has also written on the American Civil Rights Movement; at the request of The Episcopal Church, he authored the Litany of Offense and Apology in poetry and prose for the national Day of Repentance (October 4, 2008) when The Episcopal Church formally apologized, with the presiding bishop officiating, for its role in transatlantic slavery and related evils; the piece is one of several works constituting the *J. Chester Johnson Collection* in the Civil Rights Archives at Queens College (New York City). Johnson has read his work at Harvard University, the National Cathedral and on the BBC. To learn more, visit Johnson's poetry website: www.jchesterjohnson.com.

J. Chester Johnson, born in Chattanooga, Tennessee, spent his youth in Monticello, Arkansas, a small town located on the cusp of the Mississippi River Delta in southeast Arkansas. He has lived most of his adult life in New York City and is married to Freda Stern Johnson; they have two children. For over three decades, in addition to his writing, Johnson owned and ran a financial advisory firm that concentrated on debt management for states, large local governments and public authorities; he also served as Deputy Assistant Secretary of the U. S. Treasury Department during the Carter Administration. Johnson was educated at Harvard College and the University of Arkansas (Distinguished Alumnus Award, 2010).